ECONOMICS AND THE ENVIRONMENT:

ECODETECTIVES

PERC

NCEE

National Council on Economic Education

*This publication was made possible through funding from
the Calvin K. Kazanjian Economics Foundation.*

AUTHORS

John S. Morton
Vice President for Program Development
National Council on Economic Education

Mark C. Schug
Professor of Curriculum and Instruction and Director of the Center for Economic Education
The University of Wisconsin-Milwaukee

Donald R. Wentworth
Professor of Economics
Pacific Lutheran University
Tacoma, Washington

Richard D. Western
Center for Economic Education
The University of Wisconsin-Milwaukee

Cover photos: © **Zoran Milich / Masterfile,** © **Ron Fehling / Masterfile,**
© **David Muir / Masterfile,** © **Carl Valiquet / Masterfile and** © **Daryl Benson / Masterfile**

ISBN: 1-56183-574-9

Contents

CONTENTS

FOREWORD

The National Council on Economic Education (NCEE) is pleased to present *Economics and the Environment: EcoDetectives,* a set of 15 lessons intended for use in middle school and high school courses or units in environmental education. We believe *EcoDetectives* will make an important contribution to the field, helping today's young people gain the insights and skills they will need to address environmental issues effectively in their role as citizens.

Interest in environmental quality has grown steadily in recent years. The media regularly feature reports and commentary on issues related to endangered species, resource depletion, land use, and air and water quality. At the national and state levels, legislators and other officials find themselves occupied as never before with environmental issues. The schools have been similarly influenced. Environmental education is now an important area of study in most school programs throughout the United States.

In addressing environmental issues, teachers often can count on a high degree of interest and strong feelings among their students. Many young people respond with genuine concern to information and images that highlight environmental problems. The challenge for teachers is to move beyond that starting point, helping their students gain a well-informed approach to reasoning about environmental problems. That is the goal of *EcoDetectives.*

As a curricular document, *EcoDetectives* is distinctive for its solid grounding in economic principles. These principles are introduced in an essay by Richard Stroup, professor of economics at Montana State University and a senior fellow of the Property and Environment Research Center (PERC). In the lessons that follow, the principles Stroup introduces are condensed and represented as six principles of EcoDetection. Students draw on the principles of EcoDetection as they investigate environmental mysteries throughout the 15 lessons. The mysteries are provocatively formulated, and the instructional activities that accompany them will challenge students continually to think in new ways. Thanks to the *EcoDetectives* authors — John Morton, Mark Schug, Don Wentworth and Richard Western — for their work on these lessons.

The NCEE is grateful to PERC, the Property and Environment Research Center, for its support of *EcoDetectives.* Jane S. Shaw, PERC Senior fellow, has been a strong advocate for the project from the start and has provided thoughtful commentary on early drafts of the manuscript as the project evolved. In addition, some *EcoDetectives* lessons are based on data and analyses presented originally in PERC publications. We extend particular thanks to the authors of these publications: Daniel K. Benjamin, Holly L. Fretwell, J. Bishop Grewell, Indur Goklany, Wallace Kaufman, Kris Kumlien, Linda E. Platts, Roger Sedjo and Richard L. Stroup.

Robert F. Duvall, President and CEO
National Council on Economic Education

INTRODUCTION

Economics and the Environment: EcoDetectives is a 15-lesson curriculum designed to show how teachers and students can use economic reasoning in efforts to describe and explain important environmental problems.

The *EcoDetectives* lessons differ in form and content from the materials found in many environmental education programs. They call for investigations into 15 EcoMysteries — environmental problems or conditions that seem to be puzzling. For each EcoMystery, the investigation that follows is informed by one or more of six principles of EcoDetection. These principles are derived in turn from basic concepts of economics. In each lesson, the link to economic concepts is signaled by a list of content standards. These standards are drawn from *Voluntary National Content Standards in Economics* (National Council on Economic Education, 1997). Approaching EcoMysteries via the NCEE standards and the principles of EcoDetection challenges students to proceed on the basis of disciplinary understanding, not sentiment or commonplace assumptions.

The results of the investigations may prove to be surprising. We hope that will be the case. We have tried to infuse the lessons with ideas and inquiry strategies that will cause students to reevaluate their preconceptions and the conventional views typically associated with environmental education. Our goal is not to make students more or less committed to environmental protection. It is to show how economics can be used to gain insight into the causes of environmental problems and how, in light of such insight, we might develop effective policy responses to the problems. It is one thing to be passionate about protecting the environment. It is another to go about it intelligently.

For educators new to *EcoDetectives*, much will depend upon a solid understanding of the principles of EcoDetection it features. The principles are introduced in Lesson 1. To provide additional background, however, we include here an essay by Richard L. Stroup, professor of economics at Montana State University. The essay, adapted from a chapter in one of Stroup's books (*Eco-nomics: What Everyone Should Know about Economics and the Environment* [Washington, D.C.: Cato Institute, 2003]), states 10 principles of economics and discusses them in response to commonly-asked questions about environmental issues. The themes emphasized in Stroup's essay are reflected in the principles of EcoDetection and are drawn upon throughout

EcoDetectives. We recommend the essay, accordingly, as a starting point.

From "Scarcity: An Economics Primer," by Richard L. Stroup. Reproduced with permission from the Cato Institute.

1. In a land as rich as the United States, why do we face so many difficult choices about the environment?

Scarcity, even in a nation as wealthy as the United States, is always with us, so choices must be made.

We have vast forests in this country, but not enough to provide all of the wood, all of the wilderness, and all of the accessible recreation that we want. As soon as we log trees, build roads, or improve trails and campsites, we lose some wilderness. Similarly, we have large amounts of fresh water, but if we use water to grow rice in California, the water consumed cannot be used to supply drinking water in California cities. If we use fire to help a forest renew itself, we will have air pollution downwind while the fire burns. We have many goals, so we have to make choices about how to allocate our limited resources. The cost of these choices is what we give up — the cost of opportunities lost.

Trouble is, people have differing goals and disagree about which choice is the best one. Pursuit of differing goals may lead to conflict. Nowhere is this clearer than in environmental matters.

Consider an example. California's San Bernardino County was about to build a new hospital. Less than 24 hours before groundbreaking, the U.S. Fish and Wildlife Service announced that the Delhi Sands Flower-Loving Fly, which had been found on the site, was an endangered species. So the county had to spend $4.5 million to move the hospital 250 feet to give the flies a few acres to live on and a corridor to the nearby sand dunes. The county also had to divert funds from its medical mission to pay for biological studies of the fly.[1]

Environmentalists who want biological diversity were relieved that the hospital would move, but county officials were upset at the delay and the high cost that its hospital budget and the taxpayers would have to bear. To use resources one way sacrifices the use of those resources for other things. There is no escaping cost.

San Bernardino County faced a choice between timely provision of a health care facility and protection of a unique species. Often the choices are between different environmental goals. Our old-growth forests can be preserved, but that means giving up the enhanced recreation and wildlife appreciation that trails and campsites bring for many people. Strict preservation (which is what a wilderness designation means) also means that trees can't be thinned to minimize insect infestations and potentially catastrophic fires. In that case, the choice could be between keeping old-growth trees standing — until the next fire — or cutting some of them down so that more of them will be saved in the long run.

Scarcity is a fundamental fact of life, not just of economics. It is always present in nature, even when human beings are not. Each population of a species can flourish and expand only until it reaches the limit of available habitat, sunlight, water, and nutrients. Trees grow taller as they compete for sunlight. Some plants spread their leaves horizontally, capturing sunlight while blocking access for other species that might sprout up to compete for water and nutrients. Each successful strategy captures resources, taking them from certain competing species populations.

Competition implies that some species will lose out. The losses can happen slowly over time as change occurs. When a niche in the habitat changes, each population, using a different strategy, gains or loses relative to its competitors. Even small changes in a habitat can change the competitive outcome and reallocate space, water, and nutrients among populations of various species. Every change in a local environment will favor some species at the expense of others. And local environments are always changing over time, whether humans are present or not.

In other words, scarcity and competition are normal conditions in the world, not harmful ideas introduced by selfish human beings.

2. Even though economists emphasize selfish motives, don't people have common goals? Doesn't everyone want a safe and attractive environment?

People share many values, but each person has a narrow focus and somewhat different purposes; each person wants to emphasize different goals.

The goals of some individuals are selfish — intended to further only their own welfare. The goals of others are altruistic — intended to help their fellowman. In either case, each individual's concerns and vision are focused mainly on a narrow set of goals.

Even the most noble and altruistic goals are typically narrow. Consider a couple of famous examples. The

concern felt by the late Mother Teresa for the indigent and the sick of Calcutta was legendary. So, too, was Sierra Club founder John Muir's love of wilderness and his focus on protecting wilderness for all time. The goals in both cases have been widely regarded as noble and altruistic, not narrowly selfish.

Yet one might be tempted to consider that Mother Teresa would have been willing to sacrifice some of the remaining wilderness in India in order to provide another hospital for the people she cared so much about — those dying in Calcutta. And John Muir would have been willing to see fewer hospitals if that helped preserve wilderness. Individuals with unselfish goals, like all others, are narrowly focused. Each individual is willing to see sacrifices made in other less important goals in order to further his or her own narrow purposes.

As Adam Smith, the founder of classical economics, pointed out more than 200 years ago, we know and care most about things that directly affect us, our immediate family, and others close to us. We know much less about things that mostly affect people we never see. When a person furthers his or her narrow set of goals, it doesn't mean that the individual cares nothing about others. It just means that for each of us, our strongest interests are narrowly focused. These narrow sets of goals, whatever the mix of selfishness and altruism, correspond to what economists call the "self-interest" of the individuals in question.

It is unavoidable that an individual's choices will be driven by a narrow focus. Thus, people who call themselves environmentalists may differ from others who place a higher priority on providing good schools or hospitals or making sure that poor people are well provided for. And they may also differ on which environmental goals to pursue. There are thousands of worthy environmental goals, but each competes with others for our limited land, water, and other resources. Even without selfishness, the narrow focus of individuals is enough to ensure that there will be strong disagreements and competition for scarce resources.

This narrowness of emphasis is important for understanding the economics of environmental issues. Depending on the circumstances, narrow goals can lead to tunnel vision, with destructive results, or to satisfying exchanges that make all participants better off.

3. Public ownership leads to the best care of the environment — right?

Wrong! Private ownership and protection of property rights provide each resource owner with both the means and the incentive to protect and conserve the resource.

Very simply, property rights hold people accountable. When people treat property negligently or carelessly, its value decreases. When they treat it with care, its value increases. Aristotle recognized this point more than 2,000 years ago when he said, "What is common to many is taken least care of, for all men have greater regard for what is their own than for what they possess in common with others."[2] Protecting property rights helps protect the environment.

This protection is provided through the courts. In the United States, Canada, and other nations having legal roots in Great Britain, the courts have for centuries provided a way to stop individuals from injuring others by polluting. When a pollution victim shows that harm has been done or that serious harm is threatened, courts can force compensation or issue an injunction to stop the polluting activity. Such court suits are sometimes called private law but, more generally, common law. Common law refers to the body of legal rules and traditions that have been developed over time through court decisions. Each decision helps to settle the details of the law, putting everyone on notice of what is expected, reducing uncertainty and thus the need for future legal action.

It is easy to find examples of common-law protection against pollution, even going back more than 100 years. In the late nineteenth century, the Carmichael family owned a 45-acre farm in Texas, with a stream running through it, that bordered on the state of Arkansas.[3] The city of Texarkana, Arkansas, built a sewerage system that deposited sewage in the river in front of the Carmichaels' home. They sued the city in federal court on the grounds that their family and livestock no longer were able to use the river and possibly were exposed to disease.

The court awarded damages to the Carmichaels and granted an injunction against the city, forcing it to stop the harmful dumping. Even though the city of Texarkana was operating properly under state law in building a sewer system, it could not foul the water used by the Carmichaels. Indeed, the judge noted, "I have failed to find a single well-considered case where the American courts have not granted relief under circumstances such as are alleged in this bill against the city."[4]

Another example of the protection of natural resources through the protection of property rights can be found in England and Scotland. There, in contrast to the United States, fishing rights along the banks of streams are privately owned by landowners along the streams. These rights to fish can be sold or leased, even though the water itself is not privately owned.

Owners of fishing rights can take polluters of streams to court if the pollution harms their fishing rights. Indeed, after an association of anglers won a celebrated case in the early 1950s against a government-owned utility and a private firm, it has only rarely been necessary to go to court to stop pollution that damages fishing. Once established by precedent, such rights seldom need to be defended in court unless in a particular case the circumstances are new and unlike previous cases. When the courts are doing their job in protecting property rights, natural resources are protected more effectively than by extensive bureaucratic controls such as contemporary environmental regulations.

The tradition that protected the Carmichaels in the nineteenth century still protects citizens today. However, in many cases, these common-law rules have been superseded by government regulations. For example, the City of Milwaukee in 1972 tried to sue the state of Illinois for polluting its water. But the passage of the Clean Water Act in 1972 led a judge to dismiss the case because water pollution was now in the hands of federal agencies.[5]

4. Why do fierce arguments between organizations and individuals erupt over decisions about our resources and environment?

Although scarcity guarantees competition, some forms of competition lead to constructive action that reduces scarcity, while other forms are destructive.

Disagreement on values is normal. Some environmentalists who strongly appreciate the recreational and aesthetic benefits of wild, free-flowing rivers propose that dams be removed around the nation. Other people who value the flood protection, recreation, and clean hydropower provided by the dams want to preserve them. Similarly, wilderness advocates lobby to prevent the construction of new roads in roadless areas, while people who want greater public access to the same lands lobby for additional roads and campgrounds.

The same lands and rivers cannot simultaneously provide the advantages of preservation in a wild state and the benefits of development to improve access and the delivery of other services. Competition over the management of these rivers and lands is inevitable. The only question is the form that competition will take.

Human competition can be violent or it can be peaceful and constructive. Markets are generally peaceful. Even the repellent term "cutthroat competition" refers to a constructive activity. It means offering buyers low prices in order to get them to buy something. Sellers compete for buyers by improving their products and lowering their costs.

Human competition can also be destructive. Wars are the prime example, of course, but competition can be destructive even when it is not violent. Political battles, for example, can result in costly and expensive smear campaigns by various sides, each seeking to take votes from the other.

5. As people seek to meet their goals, can we predict how they will choose among the many ways in which they can advance those goals?

Yes. Incentives matter.

Nearly everyone would want to save a person who is drowning. But each of us is more likely to try to rescue a person who falls into two feet of water at the edge of a small pond than to try to rescue someone who falls over the edge of Niagara Falls. In other words, whatever the goal, we can predict that people will more likely act to achieve it when the cost to them is minimal, and will seek low-cost ways — low cost to themselves and their goals — to do so. These costs and benefits — or penalties and rewards — are called incentives.

Incentives help us to understand behavior. If a person's goal is to increase his or her income, that person has an incentive to devote long hours to a grueling job. If federal taxpayers can help pay the cost of a highway in one state, the state legislature has an additional incentive to build the highway. If people can protect an endangered species without disrupting their lives, they are more likely to choose to save it.

Incentives also affect the methods people use to achieve a particular goal. For example, to generate electricity from burning coal requires water for cooling. But how much water? Evaporative cooling consumes more water than coolers that work like a car radiator, recirculating the water. But using more water by evaporating it can get more electricity from the same coal. Where water is more expensive, generating companies will probably choose to use more coal and less water by using recirculating cooling methods. But where water is cheaper,

generators will use more water, evaporating it into air, and save on coal. Operating steam-electric power plants can use as little as 1.3 gallons of water to generate a kilowatt-hour of electricity, or as much as 170 gallons, depending on the relative cost of water.

It is not difficult for us as individuals to recognize and evaluate the cost of different choices. We are well-tuned to the relative costs we face in choosing among the available alternatives. However, it's more difficult to recognize and take into account the costs facing others. Costs to others will have less effect on our choices than the costs — and benefits — that we incur directly.

Typically, we expect people in business or individuals seeking personal goals to be more sensitive to their own costs than to those of others. We sometimes assume that government officials will behave differently. But a well-known court case brought by South Carolina developer David Lucas shows that officials of South Carolina were also more sensitive to their own costs than to those of their constituents.[6]

The saga began when the state passed a law regulating construction along its coastline, presumably to preserve open space and to prevent possible erosion. David Lucas owned two lots along the shore, but once the law was passed, officials told him that he could not build there, even though people next to his property had already built homes on their shoreline properties.

As a result, Lucas lost nearly all the value of his land. He believed that if the state wanted to control his land for a public purpose (other than stopping him from harming other people or property), the state should pay for it. So he sued to force payment. Initially, Lucas lost, but he appealed all the way to the U.S. Supreme Court and finally won. The court told South Carolina that it must pay for the land because it had taken from Lucas the same rights to use it that his neighbors enjoyed.

Once the state was faced with having to pay Lucas more than $1 million, officials changed their minds about keeping the land from development. In fact, the state sold the land to a developer!

Earlier, when they thought Lucas would pay the cost of stopping development, state regulators had little incentive to worry about the cost. But when forced to bear the cost from their own budget, they made the opposite decision: They allowed development. Incentives mattered.

The Endangered Species Act illustrates the harm that can occur when one party (in this case, the government) determines how another (in this case, landowners) must use land. Under the act, government officials have great latitude in telling landowners what to do if they find an endangered animal such as a red-cockaded woodpecker on their properties. The government chooses the protection methods, but the landowner must pay the costs. For example, the owner may not be allowed to log land within a certain distance of the bird's colony. In some cases, government officials have prevented discing (that is, plowing up land to create a firebreak) and even farming. With this power, the government is likely to be lavishly wasteful of some resources (such as land) while ignoring other ways of protecting the species (such as building nest boxes). To the government agency, the land is almost a free good.

The point of these two examples is that when people have to pay for what they use, they carefully weigh the costs and benefits.

Although incentives are important, they are not the only factors in decision making. For example, income levels affect how people deal with environmental problems. People with high incomes tend to have more concern about the protection of natural environments, such as old-growth timber or the habitat for rare plants or animals. Those with lower incomes frequently want to see those same lands managed to produce more food, raw materials, and jobs. Very poor people, wanting the basics of environmental protection such as drinking water free of parasites and microbial diseases in order to stay alive, may not be able to go much beyond that to effect environmental quality, even if given some incentive to do so. The same incentive may not have the same effect on people in difference circumstances.

Other factors matter, too. Cultural norms and traditions affect how people value various parts of their environment. Whether people toss litter on the ground or out of a car window reflects their education and probably the attitudes of those with whom they associate.

6. In market exchange, people can only gain at the expense of others — right?

Wrong! Voluntary exchange — that is, market trading — creates wealth.

It's amazing but true that simple voluntary exchange can create wealth. Both sides can gain. One way to understand this principle is to think about something that people really disagree about—say, music. John likes opera. Jane likes rock music. If John has a rock concert ticket and Jane an opera ticket, just exchanging the tickets will make each person wealthier.

Trade can create value in three ways:

1. Trade channels resources, products, and services from those who value them less to those who value them more. Without any change in production, the trade of the opera ticket for the rock concert ticket produces value.

2. Trade enables individuals to direct their resources to the activities where they produce the greatest value so that they can then trade the fruits of those activities for the items they want for themselves. The farmer in central Montana who grows wheat produces far more than he wants to consume. He trades the wheat for income to buy coffee from Guatemala, shoes from Thailand, and oranges from Florida. The Montana farmer might have been able to grow oranges, but given the cold Montana climate, doing so would have squandered resources. Trade enables people to obtain many things they would not have the proper talent or resources to produce efficiently themselves.

3. Trade enables everyone to gain from the division of labor and from economies of scale. Only with trade can individuals specialize narrowly in computer programming, writing books, or playing professional golf — developing highly productive skills that would be impossible to obtain if each family had to produce everything for itself. Similarly, the sales of large automobile factories that bring the cost of cars within reach of the average worker would not be feasible without large-scale trade that enables the product of one factory to be sold in a wide market area.

Resource owners gain by trading in three different ways: across uses (for example, out of low-valued crops into ones that earn more money), across space (marketing products across geographic distance to different states or nations), and across time (gaining from conservation or speculation by saving resources until they become more valuable).

Many farmers in the western United States own rights to divert and use water from streams to produce crops. In recent years, more people have been seeking high-quality streams for fly-fishing. They recognize that many streams have a tendency to dry up in hot summer

INTRODUCTION

months when farmers divert large amounts of water for their fields. These fly-fishers may want more water kept in streams to keep fish thriving. To keep the streams full of water, some fishers are willing to trade cash for the farmers' water rights. And some farmers are happy to part with a portion of the water they have been using in exchange for cash.

Exchanges of this sort are being carried out in Oregon. Andrew Purkey of the Oregon Water Trust works out trades between his organization, which is committed to protecting salmon, and farmers who are willing to give up some of their water. For example, Purkey paid a rancher $6,000 to not grow hay one year. The water the rancher would have used stayed in the stream and supported the fish.

Other farmers might gain by selling some of their water rights to growing cities, which can then save the cost (and the environmental disturbance) of building another dam — or a saltwater desalinization plant to make fresh water from ocean water. When such trades among willing buyers and willing sellers are allowed by law, both buyer and seller are made better off. Value is added to the water's use. Wealth is created. Unfortunately, right now the federal government and many Western states have laws that pose obstacles to trade in water. These obstacles, such as the rule that only some uses of water are allowed, tend to keep water in agriculture, reducing efficient use and conservation.

Even trade in garbage can create wealth. Consider a city that disposes of garbage in a landfill. If the city is located in an area where underground water lies near the surface, disposing of garbage is dangerous, and very costly measures would have to be taken to protect the water from leakage. Such a city may gain by finding a trading partner with more suitable land where a properly constructed landfill does not threaten to pollute water. Such a landowner may be willing to accept garbage in return for pay. If so, both parties will be better off.

7. Information is the resource of the modern age; every decision should be made with full information. Right?

Wrong again! Information is a valuable, but costly, resource.

Let's say that a private owner decides to build a landfill for garbage. The owner is liable for damages if waste deposited in the landfill leaks out and harms others. So the owner must decide how to prevent leaks and how to

clean them up if they occur. Spending too little on preventing harm from escaping pollutants could bring costly lawsuits. But spending more than is necessary imposes needless costs and wastes resources. How many resources should be devoted to preventing harm? In other words, how much should be spent? That is the decision facing the owner.

To make the decision, good information is crucial. Yet gathering more information (Where is the groundwater underneath this land? How effective will a clay cap be? What liner will be the safest?) to make a better decision is also costly.

The owner, operating in the private sector, has an incentive to gather just enough information — not too much and not too little — because both the costs and the benefits of seeking more information fall upon the owner. Weighing the costs and benefits of more information, the owner won't end up with perfect or complete information but will make a reasonable choice based on the costs and benefits of seeking more knowledge.

Now suppose that a government regulator (perhaps someone in the local zoning office) has the authority to decide whether the landfill can be built. This individual's desire for information will be much different. If damage occurs, the regulator could be blamed, so his or her incentive will be to require as much information as possible before allowing the landfill to be built. Further, the regulator doesn't face the costs of seeking more information or the costs of choosing the most expensive way to reduce risks from the landfill. The regulator may ask for study after study to make sure that the proposed landfill will really be safe. Not surprisingly, people running small businesses often complain that regulators are simply asking for too much paperwork.

In other words, the information-gathering process is affected by where the costs fall. A regulator might demand too much information, but under some conditions the owner might seek too little. Suppose the property rights of neighbors are not effectively protected under law, and the private owner of the waste site is not accountable for harm caused by materials escaping from the site. In that case, the owner may minimize the cost of preventing pollutants from seeping out of the site, trusting that the costs of the harm will fall on others. The incentive to seek additional information is weak because the owner doesn't expect to pay the costs of making a poor decision.

Important decisions require good information. Should

a forest be cut now and replanted? Should the owner of a potentially polluting hazardous waste site be forced to spend several million dollars in a cleanup effort? Should mineral exploration for new mineral deposits be conducted now or later? Should an environmental rule be further tightened?

Each of these decisions involves gathering scarce and costly information, and each decision must be made without complete information. But the information-gathering process will be shaped by the incentives facing the decision maker.

8. New technology may be cheaper, but doesn't it destroy the environment? Wouldn't we be better off, environmentally, if only older, tried-and-true technologies were allowed?

No. Advanced technologies typically help the environment because they decrease resource waste and increase resource productivity.

Sometimes we wish for the good old days before we suffered from the pollution and congestion caused by automobiles. But our ancestors didn't think of cars that way. To them, the advent of the automobile was a blessing since it meant that horses no longer clogged the streets with horse manure. And today, thousands, perhaps millions, of acres have reverted to forest because the land is no longer devoted to growing grass and hay for horses. Also, new farming technologies allow for more production from fewer acres, freeing still more land for reversion to habitat and recreation.

Yes, the automobile does pollute. But today's cars emit a tiny fraction of the pollution emitted by the cars of the early 1970s. And while even very expensive and clean-running electric cars require energy from burning fuel in power plants, the emissions from such plants have gone down drastically, too, as owners have searched out low-sulfur coal and technical devices to reduce pollution. Advances in technology continue to make cars cleaner and safer, just as diesel train engines replaced dirty steam locomotives, and gas and electricity replaced coal for home heating.

New technology is almost always adopted because it is more efficient. It usually uses fewer resources to produce the same result. Stifling new technology unnecessarily forces us to forgo additional gains that could be delivered over time.

9. If the rich countries would just stop consuming so much, couldn't we all live more comfortably on this planet?

No. As people's incomes increase, their willingness to pay for protecting the environment increases.

Even poor communities are willing to make sacrifices for some basic components of environmental protection, such as access to safe and clean drinking water and sanitary handling of human and animal wastes. As incomes rise, citizens raise their environmental goals. Once basic demands for food, clothing, and shelter are met, people demand cleaner air, cleaner streams, more outdoor recreation, and the protection of wild lands. With higher incomes, citizens place higher priorities on environmental objectives.

The connection of income with better environmental quality has often been noted by economists. One study, for example, showed that in countries where rising incomes reached about $6,000 to $8,000 per year in 2001 dollars and where there initially was an increase in certain types of air pollution, air pollution began to decline.[7] Also, the kinds of water and air pollution (indoor air pollution and water with parasites or microorganisms) that very poor people confront fell steadily with rising incomes.

Another study suggests that the willingness of citizens to spend and sacrifice for a better environment rises far faster than income itself increases — more than twice as fast, according to recent economic research.[8] (That same willingness and ability to pay for a better environment falls with falling income.) The fact that readers of *Sierra* magazine (most of whom are members of the Sierra Club) have incomes almost twice as high as that of average Americans is another indicator that there is a link between income and active concern about environmental matters.

One implication of this link is that the wealthier the people of North America, the more concerned about the environment they will be. Similarly, if incomes fall, people will be less interested in environmental protection. Policymakers should also recognize that if improvement in environmental quality can be achieved at a lower cost — rather than wasted through bureaucratic red tape, for example — public support for additional environmental measures will be greater. Policies that do not deliver good environmental quality at the least cost to the economy needlessly reduce the citizens' willingness and ability to pay for environmental quality measures.

10. What is the single most common error in thinking about the economics of environmental policy?

INTRODUCTION

The most common error in economics, as in ecology, is to ignore the secondary effects and long-term consequences of an action.

It is easy to overlook the unintended side effects of an action, especially if those effects will not be experienced soon. When individuals are not personally accountable for the full costs of their actions, they tend to ignore the secondary costs of what they do.

Consider the classic case of overgrazing on a commons, a pasture open to all herdsmen for cattle grazing. Each herdsman captures the immediate benefits of grazing another cow, but may hardly be aware of the reduction in next year's grass that the extra animal grazing this year is causing. The individual herdsman is forced to bear only a fraction of the costs — the reduced grazing available next year due to excessive grazing now — because all users share the future costs. If the herdsman removed his cow, he would bear fully the burden of reducing his use. Thus, each herdsman has an incentive to add cows, even though the pasture may be gradually deteriorating as a result. This situation is known as the tragedy of the commons.

A similar problem can occur when a fishing territory is open to all fishers. Each fisher captures all the benefits of harvesting more fish now, while paying only a small part of the future costs — the reduction of the fish population for future harvest. It is easy to ignore the indirect costs that will occur in the future, especially if the fisher will not ultimately pay the full, true cost of his or her actions.

Government decision making provides additional examples. It is typical for cities to be years behind in the maintenance of their water-delivery systems. The cost of a repair that will reduce water leaks is borne now, while much of the benefit lies in the future. The present costs tend to be more vividly seen and felt than the future benefits, so repairs are often postponed, even though the delay will make the future costs much larger.

CONCLUSION

These 10 points provide a basis for understanding how economics applies to environmental decision making. They lay the foundation for understanding, first, how cooperation can help to protect the environment and, second, why conflict often occurs instead.

---

1   William Booth, "Flower-Loving Insect Becomes Symbol for Opponents of Endangered Species Act," *Washington Post,* April 4, 1997, A-1.

2   Aristotle, quoted by Will Durant in *The Life of Greece* (New York: Simon and Schuster, 1939), 536.

3   See Roger E. Meiners and Bruce Yandle, *The Common Law: How It Protects the Environment,* PERC Policy Series PS-13 (Bozeman, Mont.: PERC, May 1988), 4-10.

4   *Carmichael v. City of Texarkana,* 94 F. 561 (W.D. Ark, 1899) at 574.

5   Bruce Yandle, *Common Sense and Common Law for the Environment* (Lanham, Md.: Rowman & Littlefield, 1997), 109.

6   More details about the Lucas case can be found in James R. Rinehart and Jeffrey J. Pompe, "The Lucas Case and the Conflict over Property Rights," in *Land Rights: The 1990s Property Rights Rebellion,* Bruce Yandle, ed. (Lanham, Md.: Rowman & Littlefield, 1995), 67-101.

7   Gene M. Grossman and Alan B. Krueger, "Economic Growth and the Environment," *Quarterly Journal of Economics* 110, no. 2 (1995), 353-77.

8   Don Coursey, *The Demand for Environmental Quality* (St. Louis, Mo.: John M. Olin School of Business, Washington University, December 1992).

LESSON 1

THE PROBLEM OF THE HOMELESS SALMON

LESSON 1

THE PROBLEM OF THE HOMELESS SALMON

LESSON DESCRIPTION

This lesson introduces the principles of EcoDetection, a key element of *EcoDetectives*. By reference to the principles of EcoDetection, the lesson describes the problem of declining wild salmon populations and calls upon students to compare the life cycle of a wild salmon to the life cycle of a farmed salmon. The students use the principles of EcoDetection to evaluate a program to restore fish habitat and to explain the mystery of the homeless salmon.

BACKGROUND

Wild Chinook salmon spawn in riverbeds and migrate to the Pacific Ocean. They spend most of their lives there until they return home to lay eggs for a new generation. Wild salmon are valued by commercial fishers, sports fishers, biologists and environmentalists. They are an important element in the unique physical and cultural environment of the Pacific Northwest. But the population of wild salmon has been declining for decades. Private fishing organizations and agencies representing Washington, Oregon, British Columbia and the U.S. government have supplied salmon from fish hatcheries to help maintain the salmon population, but these efforts have not solved the problems affecting wild salmon. Hatchery fish are different from the native wild salmon and compete with them for food. The wild Chinook salmon are now an endangered species.

ECOMYSTERY

Why is the wild Pacific salmon population in the Pacific Northwest declining while the Atlantic salmon population in the same area is increasing?

ECONOMIC REASONING

Wild salmon suffer from the problem of common ownership and the rule of capture. They belong to no one (or everyone) until someone captures them; thus no one has an incentive to do what it would take to maintain healthy population levels (See EcoDetection principle 4 in Visual 1.3). People benefit if they harvest wild salmon, but no one benefits by holding back on harvesting, which would allow wild salmon populations to grow (EcoDetection principle 3). People also benefit from certain actions that harm salmon habitat such as building dams, raising livestock and irrigating farm lands. These actions are not undertaken to harm the salmon. They are undertaken to provide people with things they want to have. The harm to the salmon is an unintended consequence of using scarce resources in that way (EcoDetection principle 1). One way to prevent the unintended consequences would be to change the incentives involved. Private ownership of water rights and salmon-spawning beds could create a new set of incentives, helping to maintain the wild salmon population (EcoDetection principles 5 and 6).

ECONOMIC CONCEPTS

- Benefits
- Choice
- Costs
- Incentives

OBJECTIVES

Students will:

1. Identify the six principles of EcoDetection.

2. Use the principles of EcoDetection in reasoning about an environmental mystery.

3. Assess the incentives that influence people's decisions regarding protection of farmed salmon and wild salmon.

CONTENT STANDARDS

- Productive resources are limited. Therefore, people cannot have all the goods and services they want; as a result, they must choose some things and give up others. (NCEE Content Standard 1.)

- People respond predictably to positive and negative incentives. (NCEE Content Standard 4.)

- Costs of government policies sometimes exceed benefits. This may occur because of incentives facing voters, government officials, and government employees, because of actions by special interest groups that can impose costs on the general public, or because social goals other than economic efficiency are being pursued. (NCEE Content Standard 17.)

Time

60 minutes

Materials

- A transparency of Visuals 1.1, 1.2, and 1.3
- A copy of Activities 1.1, 1.2, and 1.3 for each student

Procedure

A. Welcome the students to the world of environmental mysteries. Introduce the idea that environmental problems often puzzle people. For example, everyone wants clean air, yet most people help to pollute the air when they drive their cars or ride on a bus. Most people value wild animals and fish, yet our uses of land and water sometimes cause the population of wild animals and fish to decline. Why do we find these contradictions between what we want and what we do? The mysteries posed in *EcoDetectives* invite the students to learn about these contradictions, to understand why they exist, and to propose and evaluate means of correcting the problems they imply. Lesson 1 introduces the EcoDetection process and illustrates its application to the mystery of the homeless salmon.

B. To begin their environmental investigations, the students follow the story of the Chinook and Atlantic salmon living in the Pacific Northwest (PNW). **Display Visual 1.1** and invite the students to speculate on why wild Chinook salmon populations, native to the PNW, are decreasing while the Atlantic salmon, not native to the PNW, are increasing.

C. **Distribute Activity 1.1,** which describes the habitat and life cycles of Chinook and Atlantic salmon. Ask the students to write their responses to the questions. Review their answers in a class discussion.

Answers:

Part 1:

1. Where do the Chinook salmon live?

   In the North Pacific Ocean and the rivers and streams of Alaska, British Columbia, Washington, Idaho, Oregon and northern California.

2. Where do the fingerling salmon travel?

   They leave stream beds and travel through streams and rivers to the ocean.

3. Why do the Chinook salmon leave the ocean?

   After growing to maturity, they return to the place where they were born — to leave eggs.

4. What dangers do the Chinook salmon face in returning to the rivers and streams?

   They may be harmed or killed by people, bears, other fish, nets, dams and low water.

Part 2:

1. Is the total number of farmed Atlantic salmon growing or declining? *Growing.*

2. Who protects the farmed salmon from predators? *The owners.*

3. How does the caged Atlantic salmon obtain its food? *It is fed by the owners.*

4. Is the farmed Atlantic salmon homeless?

   No. The owner provides and cares for the habitat of the fish.

D. **Display Visual 1.2,** showing the rivers of the Pacific Northwest. Trace the journey of the Chinook salmon. The Chinook that make their way to the ocean live there for several years, constantly moving. Then instinct tells them to return to their birthplace and spawn, leaving behind new eggs to produce a new generation of salmon. After spawning, the Chinook die, and their remains are eaten by eagles, crows and other scavengers.

E. Explain that salmon is a very popular fish, served in the best restaurants in the world. Many people make their living catching salmon in the high seas or at the mouths of rivers when the fish return from the ocean to spawn. Sports fishers pay very high prices to hire guides and purchase equipment in order to fish for salmon every fall in the Pacific Northwest.

F. Explain that the students' task is to propose a solution to the Northwest Power Planning Council to correct the problem of the declining wild salmon population. The Northwest Power Planning Council was established by the U. S. Congress to develop a program to protect the Columbia River Basin's fish and wildlife. Ask: How can conditions in the rivers and oceans be changed to allow the population of wild salmon to increase? Encourage a variety of responses.

G. Explain that one way to solve this problem is to apply a set of principles as a starting point for thinking logically about how to describe the problem and how to assess the evidence related to it.

H. **Display Visual 1.3**, which presents the principles of EcoDetection. Explain that this visual introduces the principles students will use to solve EcoMysteries throughout this program of study. Stress the important third assumption of EcoDetection: People's choices influence the environment. In making use of this assumption to analyze problems, EcoDetectives ask: Why do people make the choices they make? What benefits do they expect? What costs do they encounter?

I. Show how the principles of EcoDetection work by asking the students to use them in thinking about possible explanations of the salmon mystery. Ask:

1. Do fishers deliberately choose to catch so many salmon that none will be left for the fishing season next year? *No.*

2. Can fishers continue catching fish if they catch so many that none will exist after one year of fishing? *No.*

J. **Distribute Activity 1.2.** Divide the class into small groups. Explain that this activity shows how the principles of EcoDetection can be used to solve an environmental mystery. Allow the students time to read and discuss Activity 1.2, using the discussion questions as a guide. Discuss the groups' responses:

1. What human choices affect the environmental quality of the salmon's spawning areas?

   People choose to use electricity, buy paper, build homes, eat food, and so on.

2. What unintended consequences have resulted from consumers' choices to obtain food and shelter?

   The choices have encouraged producers to ignore the salmon habitat, thus reducing salmon populations.

3. What difference does it make that the salmon are wild and no one owns the right to raise and harvest them, as people do with cattle, chickens and farmed salmon?

   No one is rewarded for helping the salmon to reproduce — by protecting their breeding areas, for example. With cattle and chickens, ranchers who raise and care for the animals also benefit by selling them to consumers. The prospect of this benefit creates an incentive to raise and care for the animals.

4. What might be done to increase the wild salmon population?

   Create rights of legal ownership to create incentives that would encourage people to protect salmon habitat. If people held ownership rights to water, schools of salmon and spawning areas, then fishers and producers of electricity and lumber could negotiate deals that would allow them to protect the salmon and produce goods and services.

K. **Distribute Activity 1.3.** Allow time for the students to read the Activity and respond to the Questions for Discussion.

Answers:

1. *Yes, scarcity is shown here to influence people's choices. The ranch can be used for livestock or recreation. It has more than one valuable use.*

2. *There were at least two opportunity costs: reduced livestock production and the lost possibility of using the land for housing developments. There were also monetary costs involved in changing the habitat to make it fish- and wildlife-friendly.*

3. *Prior decisions to raise livestock in the area damaged the environmental quality of the stream. The decisions to raise livestock also meant that wildlife would find it difficult to compete for food.*

4. *The tribes are paid to care for the land and restore its environmental quality.*

5. *The Northwest Power and Conservation Council was required to soften the impact of hydropower dams on fish and wildlife. The Council purchased the land to comply with this federal requirement. Funding was provided by the Oregon Water Conservation District and the U.S. Fish and Wildlife Service, along with the Bonneville Power Administration. In the past, nobody funded such programs.*

6. The Northwest Power and Conservation Council was able to buy the ranch from a private owner and convert its use to wildlife habitat. The Confederated Tribes of the Warm Springs Reservation were retained to manage the land and protect it in a manner consistent with the owner's objective.

CLOSURE

• With the students, review the principles of EcoDetection. Stress the point that environmental problems result from human choices; therefore, environmental problems can be corrected if incentives are provided to encourage people to make environmentally friendly choices.

ASSESSMENT

Multiple-Choice Questions

1. Which of the following statements is consistent with the principles of EcoDetection?

a. The wild salmon population is declining because no one cares about the salmon.

b. The wild salmon population is declining because people use salmon for food.

c. **There are few incentives for people to preserve salmon habitat.**

d. If farmers didn't irrigate their crops, the wild salmon population would increase.

2. Which of the following groups will pay higher costs if the wild salmon population is preserved and increased?

a. Logging companies operating near salmon-spawning schools.

b. Electrical companies operating dams on rivers where wild salmon travel to spawn.

c. Consumers.

d. **All of the groups listed above will pay higher costs.**

3. Which of the following statements is consistent with the principles of EcoDetection?

a. Farmed salmon are better-tasting than wild salmon.

b. **Owners of farmed salmon are rewarded for protecting the environment of the fish they own.**

c. Creating and enforcing rules that forbid farmed fish from escaping into the wild will not have any impact on decisions made by fish farmers.

d. Canadians have more fish farms because they are less interested in the wild salmon.

Essay Questions

1. Explain how incentives influence human behavior toward salmon and contribute to the decline in wild salmon populations.

People are rewarded for harvesting salmon. They are not rewarded for helping new salmon hatch and grow to maturity. Therefore, people spend more time and resources harvesting salmon than they do helping salmon populations grow.

2. Use EcoDetectives principle 4 to respond to the following statement:

"I don't see why people are worried about salmon fish farms. They will not survive the competition with wild salmon. If all you have to do is go catch free salmon in the ocean, who would want to go to the trouble of running a fish farm?"

Fish farmers are compensated for the cost of caring for fish. For many of them, the benefits of fish farming outweigh the costs. As long as that relationship exists, fish farming will continue to grow as an industry. Furthermore, salmon caught in the ocean do not come free. People who fish for salmon in the ocean pay for boats, fuel, equipment, and other costs.

VISUAL 1.1

THE MYSTERY OF THE STRUGGLING CHINOOK AND THE THRIVING ATLANTIC SALMON

The population of wild Chinook salmon, native to Pacific Ocean coastal waters, is declining while the population of non-native Atlantic salmon is increasing in the same area. What would cause this unexpected population shift?

VISUAL 1.2

MAP OF THE COLUMBIA AND SNAKE RIVERS

VISUAL 1.3

THE PRINCIPLES OF ECODETECTION

1. Resources are scarce; therefore, people must choose.

2. People's choices involve cost.

3. People's choices influence environmental quality.

4. People's choices are influenced by incentives.

5. People create rules that influence choices and incentives.

6. People take better care of things they own and value.

ACTIVITY 1.1

LIFE CYCLES: THE WILD CHINOOK AND THE FARMED ATLANTIC SALMON

Name_____

Part 1: The Wild Chinook Salmon

The Chinook salmon live in the North Pacific Ocean and in rivers and streams in Alaska, British Columbia, Washington, Oregon, Idaho and northern California. Chinook salmon have lived in these waters for more than one million years.

The wild salmon hatch from eggs left by females in the gravel of stream beds. The females die shortly after laying the eggs. Some eggs hatch into fingerlings — young salmon. Other eggs do not hatch because of bad conditions in the stream or because they are eaten by predator fish.

The fingerling salmon must find their way to the ocean, covering hundreds of miles from streams as far inland as Idaho. Their trip to the ocean is made difficult by predators and obstacles like hydroelectric dams. Once the fingerlings reach the Pacific Ocean, they live there for three to five years, growing to maturity. The mature salmon can range from 10 to 100 pounds in weight.

At some point in their maturity, the salmon instinctively try to return home — to the exact place where they were born. If they make it back, they spawn and leave eggs to produce the next generation of wild salmon. After spawning, the adult salmon die.

Many animals as well as other fish and people like to eat salmon. For the wild salmon to survive, substantial numbers of them must avoid bears, predator fish, predator birds, fishing nets, hydroelectric dams and low-water levels in rivers and streams. If they cannot make it home or if their home has been destroyed, they will not be able to produce a new generation.

During the last 30 years, wild salmon populations have declined sharply because salmon have been blocked from reaching their spawning areas or because the spawning areas have been degraded. The graph below demonstrates the drop in salmon populations in one important habitat area, the lower Snake River in Washington State and Idaho. The graph shows a direct relationship between the completion of dams and the decline of the fish population. It also indicates how many more spring and fall Chinook salmon are needed to get the populations back to the pre-dam population levels on the river.

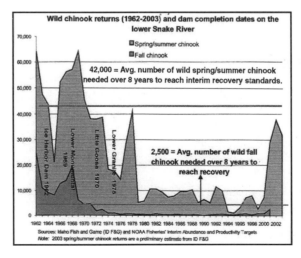

ACTIVITY 1.1, CONTINUED

Questions for Discussion

1. Where do the Chinook salmon live?

2. Where do the fingerling salmon travel?

3. Why do the Chinook salmon leave the ocean?

4. What dangers do the Chinook salmon face in returning to their home rivers and streams?

Part 2: The Farmed Atlantic Salmon

Atlantic salmon, raised in fish farms along the North American coast of the Pacific Ocean, have become a major food product worldwide. British Columbia produces over 6,590 tons of farmed Atlantic salmon annually. Farmed Atlantic salmon populations have been growing dramatically for 20 years.

A farmed Atlantic salmon begins its life as an egg produced in a private or governmental fish hatchery. The farmed salmon grow into fingerlings while living in metal cages. At some point they are transferred to large metal or mesh-net cages in the ocean. These cages are located in tidal areas near the coastline, so fresh water is naturally provided on a daily basis to help the fish live and grow.

The farmed salmon are carnivores. They must be given other fish to eat. Usually they are fed herring, mackerel, sardines and anchovies. They do not have to hunt for their food. It is provided by the owner of the fish farm.

The farmed salmon have few predators. Most owners keep the predators away from their fish nets or tanks. The owners also repair damage to the fish cages and nets so the salmon do not escape. The owners do not allow other people to disturb the salmon or harvest them.

The farmed salmon grow quickly. By their second year they are usually large enough to sell. They are butchered and sent to supermarkets where they are sold to consumers in the United States and Canada. The next generation of farmed salmon is created in fish hatcheries.

Questions for Discussion

1. Is the total number of farmed Atlantic salmon growing or declining?

2. Who protects the farmed salmon from predators?

3. How does the caged Atlantic salmon obtain its food?

4. Is the farmed Atlantic salmon homeless?

ACTIVITY 1.2

ECODETECTION AND THE MYSTERY OF THE HOMELESS SALMON

Name_____

Why is the population of wild salmon declining in the Pacific Northwest (PNW) while the population of non-native Atlantic salmon is increasing in the same area?

Most people in the PNW want the wild salmon population to increase. Wild salmon have always been an important food source in the PNW and an important element of its cultural heritage. At the same time, many people feel uneasy about growth in the population of farmed salmon. They worry about pollution created by the fish farms and about the loss of biodiversity that would be caused if farmed salmon were to escape into the wild and compete with wild fish for food and habitat. So why are the Atlantic salmon increasing in number while wild Chinook salmon populations continue to decline? The following analysis introduces the principles of EcoDetection, showing how they can be used to explain this mystery and suggest a solution to the problem.

Principle 1   Resources are scarce; therefore, people must choose.

Habitat is crucial to the survival of salmon. Salmon require abundant water. They require smaller fish to eat, and they require shallow, sandy streams in which to bury their eggs. They grow strong in the rivers and the North Pacific Ocean. They make their way inland, up the rivers, to find the right places to deposit their eggs during spawning seasons. Unfortunately, the habitat salmon need in order to reproduce can also be used for other valuable purposes. This fact makes salmon habitat scarce, no matter how abundant it may seem in some places. It is scarce because one use of it prevents other valuable uses from being realized. For example, rivers and streams can be used as sewers. Many cities and towns used rivers for this purpose until very recently. But filling rivers with urban waste degrades them as salmon habitat.

Rivers also can be used to create electricity. But hydroelectric dams make it difficult for the salmon to migrate upstream to deposit their eggs. The dams also hold water during drought years, reducing water levels and thus preventing healthy salmon runs.

Streams often run through pasture land where ranchers allow cattle to graze. If the cattle use the streams as a source of drinking water, the streams will be degraded and made unfit for salmon spawning.

The scarcity principle helps to explain why the wild salmon population has declined. Salmon habitat has more than one valuable use. Choosing one of the uses means that the other use is given up, or downgraded. Having to choose, people often have chosen uses that have been unfavorable to wild salmon.

Principle 2   People's choices involve cost.

All choices involve choosing and refusing. Or, as economists say, every choice comes with an opportunity cost. The cost is the value of the alternative not chosen. For example, in choosing to build dams, people give up other uses of a river, such as preserving it as salmon habitat. In like manner, if people choose to restore salmon runs, they will have to compensate somehow for a reduced output of electricity generated by dams. They also may have to change the behavior of livestock owners so that livestock will be prevented from disturbing spawning areas.

ACTIVITY 1.2, CONTINUED

Principle 3   People's choices influence environmental quality.

People's normal, daily behavior influences environmental quality. The decision to drive an automobile means that more car exhaust will be sent into the atmosphere. The decision to use electricity to cook a meal or power an aluminum plant means that more water must be blocked by dams, or that more power plants using fossil fuels must be built and maintained. People chose to use paper products and lumber to build homes. But logging often contributes to soil erosion, causing streams to get silted. The unintended consequences of improving the human condition can include loss of habitat for wild salmon.

Principle 4   People's choices are influenced by incentives.

Incentives are the anticipated benefits or costs (negative incentives) that may result from people's choices. In making choices, most people try to maximize the benefits and minimize the costs. If there is no reward for preserving wild salmon habitat, most people will not choose to work on that problem. But people are rewarded for creating paper products, growing livestock, creating energy and catching wild salmon for supermarket and restaurant sales. Therefore, we would expect many people — no matter how much they say they value salmon and want the numbers to increase — to use their talents for purposes other than habitat preservation.

Principle 5   People create rules that influence choices and incentives.

Communities create rules to help people live together and solve problems peacefully. In the United States and Canada, people are allowed to own land and domesticated animals. They are not allowed to own rivers or wild animals. At first glance, this seems like a commonsensical distinction, but it creates incentives that can be harmful to wild salmon. For example, since nobody can own any part of a river, nobody owned any property rights that had to be considered when dams were built on major rivers in Canada and the United States. Thus, dams could be built without regard for how they might affect previous users of the rivers — or the migrating salmon that some previous users traditionally harvested. If previous users of the rivers had owned fishing rights, as some people today own fishing rights in Great Britain, people who built dams would have been obliged to take those ownership rights into account as they planned and carried out construction projects. Migrating salmon would then have become a factor to be reckoned with. Laws and other rules influence the choices people make. Changing the rules can change the choices.

Principle 6   People take better care of things they own and value.

When people own a resource, they have a strong incentive to care for it. They receive greater rewards if they care for their possessions well. Compare wild salmon with cows or chickens or farmed salmon. Dairy farmers do not destroy their barns and let other people milk their cows free of charge. Chicken farmers do not neglect their chickens or let other people use the henhouse for an electrical switching area. Salmon farmers do not destroy the nets that hold their fish in a restricted area or let other people take their fish without compensation. Yet, in the past, wild salmon could be taken without compensation (there was no owner to compensate), and their habitat could be used in ways that no property owner would have permitted. Lumber companies were not required to restore stream habitat they damaged by logging operations. Consumers were not required to pay extra to create funds for habitat restoration. Electricity customers were not required to compensate anyone for blocking rivers with dams. Farmers irrigating their land were not required to compensate anyone for reducing the stream flows available for migrating salmon.

ACTIVITY 1.2, CONTINUED

Would the decline of the wild salmon population have occurred if someone had owned the salmon and salmon habitat? Probably not. If people had been allowed to own and benefit from the wild salmon, different choices would have been made. The salmon would not have been free for the taking, nor could their habitat have been degraded with impunity.

But how would it be possible to create ownership rights to wild salmon? How could anybody create incentives that would help to keep the salmon wild and protected? There are several possibilities. One idea is to sell water rights. How would this work? Remember that there is much competition for different uses of the water in the Columbia and Snake Rivers. The federal government could pass legislation making the use of that water a privilege that people could purchase. The government could then sell water rights along the rivers to people who want to protect the salmon (commercial and sport fishers, for example). Owners of water rights would then be able to benefit from the regulated harvest of salmon. With their property rights at stake, they could require electric companies to pay for permission to use the water. The need to compensate property owners would encourage electric companies to be conservative in using water and to consider alternative ways of producing electricity — ways less damaging to wild salmon populations. Such a change in ownership rules would change the incentives at play in the choices people make about salmon and salmon habitat. As the incentives changed, people would begin to make different choices.

Questions for Discussion

1. What human choices affect the environmental quality of the salmon's spawning areas?

2. What unintended consequences have resulted from the choices of consumers to obtain food and shelter?

3. What difference does it make that the salmon are wild and no one owns the right to raise and harvest them, as people do with cattle, chickens and farmed salmon?

4. What might be done to increase the wild salmon population?

Lesson 1

Activity 1.3

A Case in Point: Protecting the Steelhead Trout

Name_____

Directions: Read the following article and respond to the Questions for Discussion. It is an article about restoring habitat for the steelhead, an ocean-going trout. The steelhead's migration behaviors are similar to those of the wild salmon. Actions that improve steelhead habitat and populations might also work if used with salmon habitat and populations. The project described in the article is an element of the Northwest Power and Conservation Council's effort to protect habitat for wild species in the Pacific Northwest. The Council's Web site is www.nwcouncil.org. This article appears under the heading www.nwcouncil.org/fw/stories/pinecreek.htm.

Success stories — Pine Creek Ranch

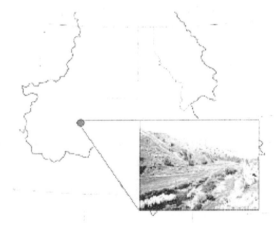

Pine Creek Ranch in north Central Oregon is being transformed steadily from cattle ranch to wildlife habitat.

Through the Northwest Power and Conservation Council's Columbia River Basin Fish and Wildlife Program, the 35,000-acre ranch was acquired in 1999 and 2001 as partial mitigation for the impacts of hydropower dams on fish and wildlife. Today the ranch is managed by the Confederated Tribes of the Warm Springs Reservation, and the once-productive habitat is being restored.

Pine Creek flows into the John Day River near Clarno, Oregon. Pine Creek Ranch includes about 10 miles of steelhead spawning and resident trout habitat on Pine Creek. Pine Creek provides spawning and rearing habitat for one of the few remaining native steelhead populations in the lower John Day River Basin. Wildlife observed on the ranch include mule deer, pronghorn antelope, Rocky Mountain elk, black bear, cougar, bobcat, mink, river otter and bighorn sheep. The ranch provides important wintering habitat for deer and elk.

Periods of uncontrolled cattle grazing, particularly along the stream banks, degraded habitat for fish and wildlife in and along Pine Creek by causing severe erosion. The erosion covered spawning gravels and decimated steelhead and trout populations, according to a 1987 report by the Wheeler Soil and Water Conservation District. The loss of streamside vegetation and the trampled banks caused by cattle, combined with flash floods caused by summer thunderstorms, resulted in deep downcutting at many places along Pine Creek — up to 10 feet in places.

LESSON 1

ACTIVITY 1.3, CONTINUED

Through their management of the ranch, the Warm Springs Tribes are improving habitat for fish and wildlife and also protecting the water, archeological and geological resources on the property. The tribes removed livestock from the damaged streamside areas and are working to control noxious weeds and juniper trees, which consume groundwater year-round.

The tribes' work follows on work already accomplished by the Conservation District. In 1987, the Governor's Watershed Enhancement Board (OWEB) funded the district to carry out a two-phase restoration project that included grazing plans, removal of juniper trees, fence construction, construction of rock structures to control erosion, willow planting along the stream banks and irrigation management.

Two examples of the restoration work are shown below (photos 1 and 2). The culvert on Pine Creek, photographed in February 2002, was a fish passage barrier and contributed to bank erosion. It was removed and replaced with three rock weirs and juniper rootwads to prevent further erosion. The culvert removal was a cooperative project between the Conservation District and the tribes, with design funding from the Oregon Watershed Enhancement Board and construction funding from the U.S. Fish and Wildlife Service and the Bonneville Power Administration, which funds the Council's fish and wildlife program.

The two photos above (3 and 4), taken from the same location on Pine Creek in 1990 and 2003, show what can happen when cattle are removed and streambanks — the riparian area — are allowed to revegetate naturally. The photo on the left was taken in 1990 by Oregon Trout and provided to OWEB to demonstrate that grazing management practices needed to change. Year-round cattle grazing was negating the benefits of an earlier habitat restoration project undertaken by the Conservation District. A subsequent management change led to better grazing practices — cattle were kept away from the creek — and allowed riparian vegetation to recover. The photo on the right shows the same location in 2003.

"This is natural growth and recovery after removal of livestock. We have seen extensive growth of riparian vegetation," said Mark Berry, the tribes' habitat manager at Pine Creek Ranch.

ACTIVITY 1.3, CONTINUED

Habitat restoration is a slow process, particularly in an arid area like north Central Oregon. While riparian areas can revegetate quickly once the damaging impacts are corrected, other elements of habitat recovery, such as improving the water table by removing junipers and noxious weeds that soak up groundwater, will take much longer, Berry said. The tribes expect fish and wildlife populations to rebound over time, but it is too soon — most of the work has been accomplished since 1999 — to see specific population increases, Berry said.

Over the long term, the ranch has potential to serve as a model for watershed recovery and wildlife habitat management in the lower John Day Basin.

Questions for Discussion

1. According to the article, does the problem of scarcity influence people's choices? Give examples.

2. What costs were involved in the choice to make the Pine Creek Ranch habitat friendlier to steelhead and trout populations?

3. How have people's choices influenced environmental quality? Give two examples.

4. What incentives encourage the Confederated Tribes of the Warm Springs Reservation to care for the wildlife habitat of Pine Creek Ranch?

5. What incentives were created to influence the choice to make Pine Creek Ranch an area for wildlife habitat instead of cattle ranching?

6. What role does ownership play in maintaining Pine Creek Ranch as a wildlife habitat?

LESSON 2

WHY DO FREE GOODS DISAPPEAR QUICKLY?

LESSON 2

WHY DO FREE GOODS DISAPPEAR QUICKLY?

LESSON DESCRIPTION

The teacher conducts a class discussion focused on how people tend to take better care of things they own and why they may be careless with things they do not own.

BACKGROUND

This lesson focuses on one important principle of EcoDetection: People take better care of the things they own and value. Because they pay the costs of ownership, people who own things also expect to receive the benefits of ownership. Because they want to receive the benefits, they generally try to use their property carefully. Many environmental problems result from lack of ownership. In situations where nobody owns the resources in question, people are not rewarded for using the resources carefully.

ECOMYSTERY

Why do free goods disappear quickly?

ECONOMIC REASONING

Private ownership of property creates incentives that encourage property owners to use resources carefully (EcoDetection principle 6). The incentives are different where property is publicly owned. Weak incentives for careful use often help to explain harmful environmental effects (EcoDetection principle 3).

In a book titled *Economics: Private and Public Choice* (The Dryden Press, 1997), James Gwartney and Richard Stroup identify four reasons why private property is often used more carefully than public property. "First, private ownership encourages wise stewardship." If private owners fail to maintain their property, it will lose value. If they do maintain it, it will gain value. "Second, private ownership encourages people to develop their property and use it productively." Productive use increases the wealth of the owners. "Third, private owners have a strong incentive to use their resources in ways that are beneficial to others." If they use their property in ways that other people find attractive, the value of their property will increase. "Fourth, private ownership promotes the wise development and conservation of resources for the future." Because private owners of forests will want future income from their land, for example, they will balance present uses of their property with future uses. That is why most forest owners replant trees; it is also why most farmers protect their soil.

On the other hand, when property is owned by government or commonly owned by a large number of people, the incentive to take care of it is weakened. For example, many people argue that public housing not well maintained. And many visitors to our public parks deplore the conditions they find there. In these cases the problem may seem to be that we do not work hard enough to maintain our public places. But the principles of EcoDetection suggest that we should expect such difficulties to persist when property is not privately owned. The difficulties persist because the incentives for protecting government property differ from the incentives that influence private owners.

ECONOMIC CONCEPTS

- Incentives
- Private property

OBJECTIVES

Students will:

1. Explain how private ownership encourages the careful use of resources.

2. Contrast the incentives created by public and private ownership of property.

CONTENT STANDARD

- Institutions evolve in market economies to help individuals and groups accomplish their goals. Banks, labor unions, corporations, legal systems, and not-for-profit organizations are examples of important institutions. A different kind of institution, clearly defined and well enforced property rights, is essential to a market economy. (NCEE Content Standard 10.)

TIME

45 minutes

MATERIALS

- A transparency of Visuals 2.1, 2.2 and 2.3
- A bag of candy with at least one piece of candy for each student

PROCEDURE

A. Explain to the class that the purpose of this lesson is to stress the relationship between private ownership of resources and the willingness to take care of those resources.

B. Take the bag of candy — perhaps M&Ms or Hershey's Kisses – and ask the students to pass the bag around the room and take what they want. Don't set any rules.

C. The bag probably won't make it all the way around the room. Some students will get no candy, and they might complain that there was enough for everyone at first. Ask why everyone didn't share the candy equally. If the class did share the candy, ask in another class why some students might have taken more than their share. The students may give many responses. Write the responses on the chalkboard, but don't evaluate them.

D. **Display Visual 2.1** and pose the mystery to the class, making reference to the candy that disappeared a moment ago. Do not try to solve the mystery at this point. Explain that today's lesson concentrates on developing a solid understanding of EcoDetection principle 6.

E. **Display Visual 2.2.** Ask:

- How do you treat a package of candy or some other treat when you are the owner?
  Expect all kinds of answers; the key point is that owners would control uses of the package and try to use it in their interest.

- Why do owners of candy companies make candy?
  They expect to benefit from owning the candy they produce. They expect to sell it eventually, thus earning income and perhaps a profit.

- Would owners of candy companies make candy if they could not benefit from ownership — if people could just take the candy without paying for it?
  No. Businesses are not charities. Business owners

expect to be rewarded for providing consumers with what they wish to have.

- What are some other ways in which candy might be distributed to the class?
  You could have charged a price for the candy or held an auction or a drawing. Evaluate the arguments presented by the students for such possibilities, but conclude that if you own the candy, you can control its use. Ownership provides rewards that encourage us to take care of property.

G. **Display Visual 2.3** and discuss the questions. Stress the contrast between private and public ownership and show that people generally take better care of things they own and value.

H. Discuss the first example given in Visual 2.3. Point out the costs and benefits of littering. People litter because it reduces their waste-disposal costs, although littering imposes costs on others. If you own the property in question, littering it would impose costs on you. You are not likely to litter — and impose costs — on yourself. Most homeowners, for example, quickly pick up litter in their yards. Values differ, of course, even among individual property owners. Some students may be sloppy, and their living rooms may look worse than the school's corridors.

I. Discuss the second example in Visual 2.3. It should reinforce the first example.

J. Discuss the third example in Visual 2.3. It is designed to suggest a slightly different concept. We generally take better care of the things we value. For example, a student may own a bicycle and a tricycle. The student doesn't care much about the tricycle because he or she no longer uses it. The bike is more important, and the student takes better care of it. Of course, the student still might want to take good care of the tricycle in order to sell it or keep it in good shape for a younger brother or sister. You could relate this point to ownership by asking the students whether they would take better care of a bike they own or a bike they might rent while on vacation.

K. Discuss the fourth example in Visual 2.3. It reinforces example three. Young people's rooms are usually messy because they don't value cleanliness as much as adults do. Nevertheless, most children do value the stuff in their rooms a lot. Things in their rooms belong to them, while the things in

LESSON 2

the rest of the house belong to others in the family. When other family members clean a child's room, they may move or throw out the child's precious possessions. In this case, other family members are not taking care of these possessions as well as the child (the owner) would.

CLOSURE

Display Visual 2.1 again and ask the students to solve the mystery.

The use of free goods (the candy getting passed around the classroom, for example) costs the user no money. If someone owns the good, he or she has to pay costs and will therefore use the good more carefully in order to preserve its value. People generally take better care of things they own because they receive rewards from ownership and also must pay the costs of ownership.

Emphasize in conclusion that the legal concept of private ownership has serious implications for protection of the environment. Private ownership is a powerful institution that may be used to enhance many environmental resources such as streams and habitat for endangered species.

ASSESSMENT

Multiple-Choice Questions

1. Why do people generally take better care of things they own and value?

   a. They are selfish and greedy.

   b. They receive the benefits of ownership.

   c. The government requires them to take care of things they own.

   d. Owners are usually rich so they can more easily afford to take care of things they own.

2. Who would most likely take the best care of a house?

   a. Private owners, because they want to increase the property's value.

   b. The government, because it cares about citizens' property.

   c. Renters, because they usually pay very high rents for the house and want to get their money's worth.

   d. A nonprofit organization, because it does not have to make a profit on the house.

Essay Questions

1. Would you expect to find more litter on a public (government-owned) beach or on a beach that is owned by a hotel?

People generally take better care of things they own and value. The hotel will lose customers if its beach is dirty. The hotel receives income from customers who use the beach, so it has an incentive to treat the beach well. Although some governments would also take good care of the beach, government agencies may have different incentives because they do not own the beach. Since the city or county government doesn't usually receive income from the users of a beach, taxpayers may not want to spend a lot of money keeping the beach clean. Monetary interests are not the only incentive, and public ownership can and does work. However, other direct controls must replace profits as an incentive if government ownership is to work.

2. Imagine a 150-acre forest of prime hardwood trees that are highly valued for use in making fine furniture. Imagine further that it will take several more years before the trees are ready to be harvested. The state government wishes to acquire the parcel of forest land and keep it in its present state as a nature preserve for camping and hiking. The owner does not wish to sell. The owner maintains that, as a private owner, he or she will take better care of this forest resource than the state government would. Evaluate the owner's claim by reference to principles of EcoDetection.

People generally take better care of things they own and value. The forest owner will benefit by receiving income from the eventual sale of the trees. The owner therefore has an incentive to preserve the trees until they are mature. Although governments may also take good care of forest land, government agencies will have different incentives. If the government agency managing the land does not benefit directly from the eventual sale of the hardwood trees, it may have an incentive to neglect the resource even though it has great value.

VISUAL 2.1

A MYSTERY AND SIX CLUES

EcoMystery

Why do free goods disappear quickly?

The Clues

1. Resources are scarce; therefore, people must choose.

2. People's choices involve cost.

3. People's choices influence environmental policy.

4. People's choices are influenced by incentives.

5. People create rules that influence choices and incentives.

6. People take better care of things they own and value.

VISUAL 2.2

WHY DID THE CANDY DISAPPEAR?

1. How do you treat a package of candy or some other treat when you are the owner?

2. Why do owners of candy companies make candy?

3. Would owners of candy companies make candy if they could not benefit from ownership — if people could just take the candy without paying for it?

4. What are some other ways in which candy might be distributed to the class?

VISUAL 2.3

YOUR SCHOOL, YOUR HOME, YOUR STUFF

1. Which is cleaner: Your school's corridors or your living room?

   Why?

2. Which is cared for better: Your kitchen (or dining room) or the school cafeteria?

   Why?

3. Which stuff that you own do you take very good care of? Which stuff that you own do you not take good care of?

   Why?

4. How does the way you clean your room differ from the way other members of your family clean your room?

   Why?

Lesson 3

Why Do We Have So Few Whales and So Many Chickens?

LESSON 3

WHY DO WE HAVE SO FEW WHALES AND SO MANY CHICKENS?

LESSON DESCRIPTION

The students participate in a classroom simulation that demonstrates the tragedy of the commons. Next, the simulation is altered by an introduction of property rights, and the simulation outcome changes. Then the students solve the mystery of the whales and chickens by comparing their simulation experiences with actual practices regarding whale and chicken management.

BACKGROUND

Commercial fishing of whales began in the seventeenth century and continued actively until the middle of the twentieth century. By that time, whale populations had dropped to very low levels. The International Whaling Commission was formed in 1946 to provide for conservation of whale stocks. It issued a ban on hunting humpback, fin and minke whales in 1986. Since then, many whale species have increased in numbers. Now whalers in Iceland, Japan and Norway want to resume hunting whales. But opponents fear that resumed whaling, even if it is limited to certain species and the killing of relatively few whales, will put whale populations in jeopardy once again.

Chickens have been raised for slaughter for centuries. Around the world, millions of chickens are killed and eaten every day. Yet despite the daily toll taken on chickens, they are in no danger of becoming extinct. In fact, the chicken population of the world seems to be increasing.

EcoMYSTERY

Under present regulations, relatively few whales are killed by whalers each year. But millions of chickens are killed and eaten every day. Yet there are too few whales, while chickens are abundant. Why are there so few whales and so many chickens?

ECONOMIC REASONING

Whaling is an activity conducted by people who do not own whales or provide care for them. The only contact whalers have with whales is to capture and kill them.

This relationship creates what economists call a tragedy of the commons — a situation in which all the incentives at play encourage people to use the resource in question, not to care for it or act to ensure its sustainability (EcoDetection principle 3).

By contrast, chickens are typically raised by owners of chickens. Owners of chickens care for their stock of chickens, managing it so that the stock is not depleted. It is in an owner's best interest to care for the chickens while they are alive and to arrange for an ongoing, fresh supply of chickens. Only by caring for chickens and maintaining a stock of them can the owner receive an adequate return for the costs involved in raising chickens (EcoDetection principle 4). Ownership, in other words, creates an incentive for people to care for what they own (EcoDetection principle 6).

No such incentives influence whalers. They are not rewarded for preserving the whale population. If one whaler, in the interests of conservation, should hold back and not take a whale, another whaler will probably take it. Lack of ownership, in other words, creates incentives that encourage harvesting whales with little or no regard for maintaining the whale population.

ECONOMIC CONCEPTS

- Choice
- Incentives
- Property rights

OBJECTIVES

Students will:

1. Participate in or observe a simulation of whaling behavior.

2. Gather data from two different simulation episodes.

3. Use principles of EcoDetection to explain the different outcomes of the simulations.

4. Suggest an appropriate answer to the mystery.

CONTENT STANDARD

- People respond predictably to positive and negative incentives. (NCEE Content Standard 4.)

TIME

60 minutes

MATERIALS

- A transparency of Visuals 3.1, 3.2, 3.3, 3.4 and 3.5
- A box of small crackers — if possible, crackers shaped like fish.

PROCEDURE

A. Explain to the students that they will investigate a controversial issue: Should people be allowed to hunt and kill whales for commercial purposes? They will also investigate a noncontroversial issue: Although millions of chickens are killed each year, no one is trying to Save the Chickens!

B. To introduce the mystery explicitly, **display Visual 3.1** and discuss it briefly with the students.

C. Ask the students to estimate the number of chicken fatalities in the United States each year. This is not as difficult as it may seem. On average, if each person in the United States eats two chickens per year, how many chickens would be killed? The population of the United States in 2000 was about 280 million people. At two chickens per person, that would come to 560 million chickens cooked up annually. And that is an estimate only for one country. China has a population of more than a billion people, and many Chinese people eat chickens, too. Obviously, many, many chickens are killed each year, yet the number of live chickens remains stable or increases.

D. **Display Visual 3.2.** Compare the case of the chicken to the case of the whale, as represented by the information on the Visual. Explain that the International Whaling Commission (IWC) recommends that a ban on killing whales of any species should remain in effect until the current population of that species returns to 54 percent of its estimated historical population (prewhale hunting). The context gets more complicated as a result of a new study done by Joe Roman and Stephen R. Palumbi. They used DNA evidence to estimate how many whales were in the historical population. Their study suggests that the IWC's estimate is too low. Both estimates represent efforts to answer an important question: When have whale populations returned to a level at which renewed whale hunting would not threaten the species? As students can see, whale population numbers indicate that whale hunting could

resume soon if the IWC's population estimates are used, whereas only minke whale hunting could begin soon if the DNA estimates are used.

E. Ask the students to consider this question: Why worry about killing whales? Killing chickens doesn't seem to threaten chicken populations. Why should killing whales threaten whale populations? Record the students' reactions on the chalkboard. Save them for later consideration.

F. Announce that the class will observe a brief activity and that you will then ask them to explain the behavior they observe.

G. Turn on the overhead projector. Scatter six to eight fish crackers on a blank transparency and adjust the projector so that seated students can see the fish. Recruit six volunteers to come to the front of the room and gather around the projector.

H. Explain to the volunteers that the fish crackers are whales, they are whalers and you are a whale buyer. You will give them two 20-second fishing rounds and will purchase any whales they bring to you in good condition. (You will not purchase whales that are crushed or broken.) For each whale caught in the first 20-second round, whalers will receive 25 cents. If any whales remain at the end of the first round, there will be a second 20-second round. If the whalers catch whales in that round and bring them to you, they will receive 50 cents for each whale. In addition, six to eight more whales will be added to the whale pod to reflect the fact that by waiting one round in the simulation, the whale hunters have allowed time for the whales to reproduce.

(Note: Consider in advance how many fish crackers to put on the screen and how much you are willing to pay for them. Generally, the fewer the whales and the older the students, the higher the pay you'll need to offer to provide an effective incentive for participation. With younger students, use individually wrapped treats or quiz points instead of coins for the reward.)

I. Immediately after you give the instructions, say "Go!" and watch the time carefully. Do not give the students time to consider the possibilities or talk over the problem before you say "Go!" (Students tend to grab the fish crackers immediately, although there may be an initial, brief hesitation until one student reaches in. Some fish may be destroyed, and typically only a few students earn money. Usually no fish are left for the second episode.)

J. Pay the students for their catch. Announce that there can be no second round because the whales are all captured or crunched. Ask the six students if they understood that the whales would have been worth more in the second round.

Usually there is no misunderstanding. If a misunderstanding does occur, run the same experiment again, particularly if no student has tried to organize the others to wait. If you decide to run it again, do so quickly. The result — grabbing, damaged fish and nothing left for the second round — will be the same.

K. Ask the whalers why they didn't wait for the second round when the whales would be worth more.

They may try to blame someone for being greedy, especially the person who grabbed first, but all will probably comment that they couldn't afford to wait for the second fishing round because they were afraid everyone else would take all the whales first.

L. **Display Visual 3.3.** Review the principles of EcoDetection briefly; then use the principles in looking back at the whaling simulation.

1. Were resources scarce?

   The whales and the time needed to harvest whales were scarce.

2. What alternatives were available to the whalers?

   To harvest now, to harvest later or not to harvest at all.

3. What choice was made among these alternatives?

   The choice to harvest immediately.

4. Did any whalers set out to destroy the whale population deliberately?

   No. Emphasize that the destruction of the whale population was not a deliberate choice, nor was it something the students considered ahead of time. It was an unintended consequence of their desire to earn income.

5. Were incentives involved in this experiment?

   Yes. Whalers were rewarded for harvesting whales. They were not rewarded for conserving whales.

6. Why didn't the whalers wait until the second round to harvest the whales? Waiting for another round would have brought higher prices and increased whale populations.

   The prospect of greater rewards later was offset by the fear that no whales would remain by the second round. No remaining whales, no incentive to wait.

7. Who owned the whales?

   Most students will respond that no one owned the whales, or everyone did. That observation is true only before the harvesting begins. After harvesting, the whale is owned by the person who grabbed it. This is called the Rule of Capture.

8. Did rules of ownership affect the incentives?

   Yes. Because ownership was unclear, everyone had an incentive to grab whales before someone else got them.

9. What caused the over-harvest of the whales?

   The incentives were structured to reward the aggressive harvester; for conservationists, there were no rewards.

M. **Place Visual 3.4 on the overhead** and place fish crackers in each property zone. Do not turn on the projector yet. Announce that you are making one change in the game. Otherwise the people and situation will remain the same. You will run the experiment again and see what happens.

N. Ask the volunteers to gather around the projector; turn on the projector so all the students can see the fish arrangement; then explain the new rule. Assign the whales in each property zone of Visual 3.4 to a student. Explain that she or he owns the whale in that property zone. Also explain that if anyone takes anyone else's whale, the thief will be fined $1, required to return the whale, and dropped from the experiment.

O. Make sure that the volunteers understand the new rule. Remind them that there will be two 20-second sessions and that the whales are worth 25 cents in the first session and 50 cents in the second session. Then say "Go!" and start timing. Call "Stop" at the end of the 20-second episode. Pay any student for his or her whale if it has been harvested carefully.

Usually, the volunteers will not harvest the whales. Some who are confused by the rules may try to harvest the whales, but the others will probably suggest it is not a good idea. If anyone takes someone else's whale, enforce the rule and take away the thief's privilege to harvest whales.

P. Start the second round. Call "Stop" at the end of 20 seconds. Pay for the harvested whales; put six more fish on the projector to demonstrate that there was time for the whales to reproduce; thank the volunteers and send them back to their seats.

Most students will carefully harvest their whales and sell them. Most likely no whales will be damaged. Don't be surprised if some students refuse to harvest their whale. They may have grown attached to it, and the small reward may not suffice as an incentive for harvesting it.

Q. **Display Visual 3.3 again.** Use the EcoDetectives principles again to analyze the second simulation activity. Note the differences between the first and second simulation activities as revealed by the analysis.

1. Were resources scarce?

   Yes. The whales and the time needed to harvest whales were scarce.

2. What alternatives were available to the whalers?

   To harvest now, to harvest later or not to harvest at all.

3. What choice was made among these alternatives?

   To harvest in the second round — very different from the first simulation.

4. Did any whalers set out to destroy the whale population deliberately?

   No. In this simulation, in fact, there would probably be an increase in the whale pod by the end of the round. The whalers probably preserved the population while they harvested from it. Emphasize that the restoration of the whale population was not a deliberate choice, nor was it something the students considered ahead of time. It was an unintended consequence of their desire to earn income.

5. Were incentives involved in this second experiment?

   Yes. Whalers were rewarded for harvesting whales in the second session. They were rewarded for conserving whales during the first round.

6. Why did the whalers wait until the second round to harvest whales?

   To get a better price. They knew they could wait for the better price because whales would still be available in the second round.

7. Who owned the whales?

   The whalers owned the whales, both before and after they harvested them.

8. Did rules of ownership affect the incentives?

   Yes. Whale ownership meant from the beginning that the whalers could wait until the whales were more valuable and had reproduced.

9. What caused the restoration of the whale population?

   The incentives were structured to reward conservation, not the aggressive harvester. This arrangement allowed the whale population to remain stable.

R. **Display Visual 3.1 again.** Ask the students to reconsider their earlier explanations. Why are there so many chickens and so few whales?

The chickens are raised by people who own them. Chicken owners take care to replenish the stock before selling off chickens for slaughter. Whalers own a whale only after harvesting it. No whaler is rewarded for conserving whales.

S. Ask the students to forecast what will happen to whale populations if nations are allowed to hunt whales again.

Under current ownership rules, the whale populations will decline at a rate depending on how fast they are harvested. No one has an incentive to increase the whale population. Different ownership policies could change that outcome.

LESSON 3

CLOSURE

Display Visual 3.5 and discuss the concept of the tragedy of the commons. Ask:

1. Which of the two simulations illustrates the tragedy of the commons?*

   The first one. Because ownership was not established until the whales were harvested, no whaler was willing to risk waiting; if anybody did wait, another whaler might take all the whales.

2. Why was there no tragedy of the commons in the second simulation?

   In the second simulation, ownership was clearly established at the outset, before any whales were harvested. And ownership rights were enforced through rules and penalties. Each owner was secure in knowing the whale would remain his or hers until the owner decided to harvest it.

* Footnote for the teacher. Why do people call this phenomenon the "tragedy" as opposed to the "sin" of the commons? It's called a tragedy rather than a sin because the consequence —the disappearance of the fish — wasn't the result of any deliberate, sinful action on anyone's part. People were engaged in pursuing beneficial activities — providing food for others to eat — without any intent to deplete the whale population.

ASSESSMENT

Multiple-Choice Questions

1. Which of the following animal populations is most likely to be threatened in a tragedy-of-the-commons slaughter?

   a. Cattle owned by a rancher in Wyoming

   b. Chickens raised by a chicken farmer in Minnesota

   c. Wild African elephants with valuable ivory tusks

   d. Dogs owned as pets by families

2. Why do commercial fishers tend to take too many fish in their efforts to harvest fish to sell to the general public?

   a. Commercial fishers are not very smart and will repeatedly act against their own interests by overfishing.

   b. Commercial fishers are rewarded for catching fish; they are not rewarded for conserving fish.

   c. Commercial fishers lack knowledge about fish populations.

   d. Commercial fishers do not have to pay property tax on the fish they catch.

Essay Questions

1. Respond to this argument:

"Fish and whale populations are threatened by the greed of commercial fishers who continue to harvest fish even when those populations are rapidly declining."

Commercial fishers are probably no more or less greedy than cattle ranchers or chicken farmers. Yet fish and whale populations are declining while cattle and chicken populations are increasing. The problem seems to be one of incentives. The fishers are rewarded only for harvesting fish or whales. The cattle or chicken owners are rewarded for taking care of their animals and maintaining an ample stock of them.

2. Many people would prefer to see wildlife remain a resource owned in common. One example has to do with loggerhead turtles that lay their eggs on the sand near beachfront property. The turtles and eggs provide excellent food for animals and humans. How can these turtles remain commonly owned and still be saved from extinction in a tragedy of the commons?

Rules must be established that provide incentives and penalties, strictly enforced, to protect the wildlife. For example, people who watch over the turtles and eggs until the new turtles are old enough to enter the ocean could be paid. If someone was caught harming the turtles or eggs, it could result in a very steep fine.

VISUAL 3.1

THE CHICKENS AND WHALES MYSTERY

A small number of whales are harvested each year, while millions of chickens are killed every day. Yet there are too few whales, and chickens are abundant.

Why are there so few whales and so many chickens?

VISUAL 3.2

WHALE POPULATION ESTIMATES

TYPE	CURRENT	HISTORIC ESTIMATE*	DNA ESTIMATE**
Humpback	10,000	20,000	240,000
Fin	56,000	30-50,000	360,000
Minke	149,000	100,000	265,000

Sources:
*The International Whaling Commission
**Joe Roman and Stephen R. Palumbi, Science, July 25, 2002

VISUAL 3.3

THE PRINCIPLES OF ECODETECTION

1. Resources are scarce; therefore, people must choose.

2. People's choices involve cost.

3. People's choices influence environmental quality.

4. People's choices are influenced by incentives.

5. People create rules that influence choices and incentives.

6. People take better care of things they own and value.

VISUAL 3.4

PROPERTY ZONES FOR WHALERS

VISUAL 3.5

THE TRAGEDY OF THE COMMONS

When property is held in common rather than owned by individuals, it tends to be overused or degraded. Each person who uses it gains the full benefit of use. However, he or she does not bear the full costs of this use. The costs are shared by all the other users — the common owners. Additionally, no one has a strong incentive to conserve resources owned in common because a person who tries to conserve the resource cannot prevent others from using it.

The tragedy of the commons is relevant to many environmental issues including the protection of whales. When whales are owned in common, whalers who kill whales gain all the benefits of their harvest; the more they kill, the more they benefit. But the aggressive whalers will bear only a small portion of the costs of their action. The cost implied by a depleted whale population will be spread out among all the common owners. In the meanwhile, if any whales are left, whalers will have no incentive to hold back. Anybody who holds back on killing whales will find that others will kill the whales instead.

LESSON 3

THE ENVIRONMENT: WHO LOVES YA, BABY?

LESSON 4

THE ENVIRONMENT: WHO LOVES YA, BABY?

LESSON DESCRIPTION

The students participate in a simulation activity that illustrates how incentives influence the behavior of people trying to earn income. In a variation of the simulation activity, they observe the effects of rule changes. When the rules change, the incentives change, and new issues of cost arise. Then the students apply a similar analysis to open-pit mining operations, taking note of a shift in costs, from internal to external, produced by new environmental regulations on mining.

BACKGROUND

Mining has been an important part of the North American economic success story. Fossil fuels and precious metals beneath the ground in Canada and the United States help provide citizens with extremely high standards of living. Yet mining can be and sometimes has been devastating to the natural environment.

Most people are in favor of taking good care of the environment. When people damage the environment, the damage most likely does not mean that anybody wants to do harm. Instead, the person doing damage is most likely responding to another incentive. One approach to correcting environmental abuse, then, is to eliminate or change the reason people have for damaging the environment in the first place. For example, if we do not want others to create open-pit mines, then we should try to change the demand for the ore supplied by open-pit mining or find a less costly way to mine ore so that open-pit mining becomes less attractive.

In 1977, the U.S. government passed the Surface Mining Control and Reclamation Act. It changed the rules for mining and motivated mining companies to treat the natural environment differently. Now miners must use methods that minimize environmental destruction and restore the environment to an acceptable level when the mining operations are complete.

ECOMYSTERY

Why do people damage the environment they love? Montana, West Virginia and the Canadian province of British Columbia boast some of the most beautiful mountains in North America. Yet in each location, open-pit mines damage the environment that most of the mine workers and owners love and use for recreation. Why do they damage the land they love?

ECONOMIC REASONING

Mining is an example of an activity people engage in even though they know it will change the environment. They choose to change the environment because they are influenced by a unique set of incentives and costs. The public's demand for coal provides income for people who extract coal ore from the earth. This income is an incentive to everyone working in the coal industry (EcoDetection principle 4). The cost of open-pit mining is lower than the cost of other types of mining that do less damage to the environment. If there is no incentive to use a less-damaging method of extraction, companies will choose to mine coal in open-pit mines (EcoDetection principle 2). New rules will change the incentives and motivate miners to change their mining practices, but the change will also change the costs for producers and consumers (EcoDetection principle 5). Before the rule change in question, citizens bore the cost as environmental damage, an external cost. After the change, citizens will bear a higher monetary cost for certain products of mining; the external cost will be internalized.

ECONOMIC CONCEPTS

- Choice
- External cost
- Incentives
- Opportunity cost

OBJECTIVES

Students will:

1. Identify the environmental damage caused by mining production.

2. Identify the opportunity cost of mining that does not disturb the surface of the earth.

3. Explain the incentives that encourage open-pit mining.

4. Evaluate the consequences of requiring miners to work without disturbing the surface of the earth.

LESSON 4

CONTENT STANDARDS

- Productive resources are limited. Therefore, people cannot have all the goods and services they want; as a result, they must choose some things and give up others. (NCEE Content Standard 1.)

- People respond predictably to positive and negative incentives. (NCEE Content Standard 4.)

TIME

45 minutes

MATERIALS

- Two clean, neatly organized classrooms with many chairs, desks and tables

- Two large containers of black beads, about the size of marbles

- A large bowl of M&M candies

- A transparency of Visuals 4.1 and 4.2

- A transparency of Visual 1.3 in Lesson 1

PROCEDURE

Before you begin: This lesson will work best if you can carry it out with another teacher and class, using two classrooms. Take special care to clean and organize each classroom before starting. Have every chair in place, every book arranged; if you can arrange to do so, place some flowers and plants in the classrooms. Gather all the students into one classroom to begin the lesson. The crowded conditions will help to make the activity successful.

A. **Display Visual 4.1.** Begin the lesson by asking the students if they like beautiful, untouched places such as mountains and forests. Encourage them to explain why they appreciate such places (usually they will comment on clean air, no trash, no loud noise, beautiful plants). Do not prolong this discussion, but collect and record some examples on the chalkboard for later discussion and comparison. Stress that nearly everyone loves the environment.

B. Explain that open-pit mining means removing the earth's surface in order to extract resources buried near the surface. Open-pit mining is often used to extract coal and iron ore. States and areas in North America with extensive mining opera-

tions include Montana, West Virginia, Wyoming, Indiana and Ohio in the United States, plus British Columbia and Alberta in Canada. Ask the students to guess why people would choose to damage the beautiful countryside in such states as West Virginia and Montana. Entertain a variety of responses: people do it for money, people are weird, people don't care about the environment, people don't know any better, and so forth.

C. **Display the principles of EcoDetection from Visual 1.3 in Lesson 1.** Remind the students that people's choices influence environmental quality and that people's choices are influenced by incentives. Explain that you are going to conduct an experiment with them that might help them solve the mining mystery.

D. Ask the students to watch carefully while you toss black beads around the room; tell them they are not to do anything until they receive further directions. Toss the beads around the room in what looks like a random fashion, but be sure to have some beads go under chairs, tables, into the plants and into other places that are difficult to reach.

E. Tell the students that they soon will have an opportunity to pick up these beads. You will give each student one M&M for every bead she or he collects in one minute. They are to work individually on this task. It is not a group activity!

F. Give the students one minute to collect beads. Be careful. The students may become noisy as they move around the room. Desks and tables may be moved as the students search for beads.

G. Calculate the total number of beads collected. Give the students M&Ms as promised.

H. In their search for beads, the students will likely have disturbed the classroom environment by pushing things aside, moving tables out of the way, and so on. Ask the students how they can justify the changes they have made to the environment of the room. Why have they made a mess of an area that was neat and well organized before they arrived?

They will probably reply that they didn't know they should keep it clean, that they tried but others destroyed it, that they didn't care because they wanted the M&Ms, or that it isn't their classroom anyway — the custodian will clean things up later.

LESSON 4

I. **Display Visual 4.2** and direct the students' attention to the definition of *incentive*. Ask the students what incentive motivated them in the search for beans.

The opportunity to gain M&M candies.

J. Now direct the students to the definition of *external cost*. Ask: Who pays the external cost of their bead-gathering activity?

Whoever has to clean the room up later. They probably figured the teacher or custodian would pick things up later and make the rooms tidy again.

K. Ask: Based on your experience gathering beads in return for M&Ms, why do you think mine owners create open-pit mines?

Income serves as an important reward for mine owners and workers. Moreover, they don't have to clean up the mess. When the mining operation is complete, they can move on to a different area.

L. Run the bead-search activity a second time, but explain to the class that no bead can be turned in for a reward this time until the area has been restored to its previous condition. The students will have one minute to search for beads and clean up the room.

M. Calculate the number of beads collected in this round and give out the M&Ms accordingly. Ask the students what the consequence was of their need to restore the environment?

Lost production of beads.

N. **Display Visual 4.2** again and direct the students to the definition of *opportunity cost*. Help the students notice that a fixed set of resources (their labor) can not be used productively for two different activities at the same time. For example, the opportunity cost of watching a TV program might be homework not done. Or the opportunity cost of babysitting on Friday night might be a pizza not enjoyed with friends. All choices involve an opportunity cost. When a company chooses to restore the environment, it bears the cost of lost production. When it produces ore by means of open-pit mining, it creates a cost borne by others — the cost of environmental harm. Every environmental action involves a cost. Usually the controversy involved in these cases comes down to who should bear the cost — the producer, the consumer or the general public?

O. Take the students to the second classroom. Again toss beads around the room and have the students collect beads for M&Ms, but this time require that they do not disturb the current environment. There will be a severe penalty (50 beads) for any disturbance of the environment, and any student caught in the act will have to restore the room to its original condition before returning to the task of collecting beads. After one minute, count the number of beads collected, give students their M&Ms and ask them to summarize how this experience is similar to the previous experience by answering the following questions:

1. What was the incentive to collect beads?

   The M&Ms

2. What was the incentive to protect the environment?

   Avoid the penalty.

3. What was the opportunity cost of protecting the environment?

   Lower collection totals than the totals in the first round in the other classroom.

4. Were there external costs in this situation?

   No, because in case of environmental damage the students would have been required to restore the original condition of the room and pay a fine. Under these circumstances, the cost of bean collecting is internalized.

CLOSURE

Explain that the U.S. government in 1977 passed the Surface Mining Control and Reclamation Act. It requires mining companies to minimize the environmental damage of their work and to restore mined areas to an acceptable level of environmental quality. Mining companies are assessed very large fines if they fail to abide by these provisions. Ask the students to use EcoDetection principle 5 to forecast the consequences of this law.

The law changes the incentives for miners. To avoid the high cost of government fines, miners will either shut down or begin to internalize the previously external costs of mining. This change will lead to lower production levels and greater amounts of land restoration. (See the Mineral Information Institute Web site for information and pictures of mine restorations at www.mii.org/rec/metals.html.)

ASSESSMENT

Multiple-Choice Questions

1. Which of the following answers does not describe an incentive to preserve the environment?

   a. Earning a "Saving the Environment" award at a job

   b. A personal love of the outdoors

   c. People will pay you to enjoy an unspoiled area you own.

   d. *A stranger complaining that "you people" are stupid to destroy your environment*

2. Which of the following examples describes an external cost?

   a. A pedestrian breathing car exhaust

   b. Fish killed when a truck accidentally spills toxic materials into a lake

   c. Airplane noise heard by school children in a school near an airport

   d. *Answers a, b, and c all describe external costs.*

3. Which of the following examples describes an opportunity cost?

   a. An environmental protester finding fault with a mining company's production methods

   b. *Funds used to purchase trees for land restoration instead of purchasing a mining drill*

   c. A mine employee driving a truck of ore to the railroad transfer station

   d. The taxes paid by the mine to fund local schools

Essay Questions

1. A paper mill in the town of Popple Creek gives off a smell like rotten eggs. An environmental group proposes a regulation that would require the mill to eliminate the smell. The mill owners object, contending that the proposed regulation would increase their costs, forcing them to raise their prices and lay off workers. The Popple Creek town council rejects the proposal, arguing that the opportunity costs of eliminating the smell are too high. The members of the environmental group do not understand the term *opportunity costs*. Write a short essay explaining the term and telling how it applies in this example.

An opportunity cost is the next-best alternative given up when a choice is made. In this case, the town council decided that group's proposal — impose a regulation in order to eliminate a bad smell — would mean that some mill workers would lose their jobs and some consumers would pay higher prices for wood products. The town council decided that that was too high a cost to pay for getting rid of a bad smell.

2. In a town meeting, a local mining company asks to expand its ore-processing operation. Local residents are in favor of the expansion, but only if the company agrees to clean up the land it has already used and restore it to a condition appropriate for wildlife habitat. The mine owner explains that he is opposed to this requirement because it will create more costs for the company. A local resident replies, "It will not increase the cost; it will just change the cost from one form to another." A friend asks you, "Aren't they contradicting each other?" How would you reply, using your economic understanding of internal and external costs?

Both individuals have a valid point. The mining company will have to pay costs it was not paying before. The local resident is also correct. The cost is already being paid in terms of the environmental eyesore and low quality of land (external costs imposed on residents) the mining operation creates. Requiring the mining company to clean up the land and restore it after mining it would make a change — shifting the cost from an external one paid by all residents to an internal cost paid by the mining company.

VISUAL 4.1

WHY DAMAGE SOMETHING WE LOVE?

Why do people damage what they love? In parts of Montana, British Columbia and West Virginia we find some of the most beautiful mountains in the North America. But we also find open-pit mines damaging the environment that most of the mine workers and mine owners love and use for their own recreation.

Why?

VISUAL 4.2

DEFINITIONS

Incentive: An anticipated reward from making a choice.

External cost: A cost paid by people who are not part of the exchange between buyer and seller.

Opportunity Cost: The next-best alternative given up when a choice is made.

CLEANING THE LAKE MARGINALLY

LESSON 5

CLEANING THE LAKE MARGINALLY

LESSON DESCRIPTION

The students examine an example of what not to do while drinking water on a long hike. They use the concept of *marginal analysis* in analyzing the example. Then they examine the marginal costs and benefits of an environmental cleanup project, using marginal analysis to find an optimal environmental solution.

BACKGROUND

Most environmental cleanup issues involve comparisons of costs and benefits. In discussing the comparisons, people typically use total costs, average costs, total benefits and average benefits to argue for the positions they take. The conversations tend to follow the same lines whether the issue at hand involves a Superfund site with serious environmental problems or a minor case of messiness in a teenager's bedroom. Underlying all these conversations, the critical question is "How clean is clean?" This lesson will show how an economist would approach such issues using marginal analysis rather than totals or averages to compare the costs and benefits of cleanup projects.

EcoMYSTERY

Everyone values clean water, and we all think we understand what *clean* means. But people often disagree about what needs to be done to clean up environmental messes. What is the problem here? Why do people disagree about something as straightforward as cleaning up an environmental mess?

ECONOMIC REASONING

Marginal analysis is critical to economic reasoning. Economics rarely deals with absolute amounts or totals. It focuses instead on what happens if a small change is made. The consequence of the next step in each case becomes the important consideration. In this manner people can assess the value of each change and make changes only when they expect that the benefit of that change will be greater than the added cost (EcoDetection principle 2). When the benefits of the next change are equal to or less than the added cost, economists would recommend that the changes cease,

whatever the relative values of average and total costs and benefits.

ECONOMIC CONCEPTS

- Marginal benefit
- Marginal cost

OBJECTIVES

Students will:

1. Define *marginal cost* and *marginal benefit*.

2. Calculate an optimal environmental cleanup level using marginal analysis.

3. Use EcoDetectives principles to explain the different outcomes of two cleanup policies.

CONTENT STANDARD

- Effective decision making requires comparing the additional costs of alternatives with the additional benefits. Most choices involve doing a little more or a little less of something; few choices are all-or-nothing decisions. (NCEE Content Standard 2.)

TIME

75 minutes

MATERIALS

- A transparency of Visuals 5.1 and 5.2
- A copy of Activities 5.1 and 5.2 for each student

PROCEDURE

A. Ask the students if they clean their own bedrooms at home. If they do, ask if their parents agree that the room is clean when the students are finished.

   Most students will indicate there is often a disagreement between the parents and the students.

B. Explain that cleanup issues divide people of all ages. Teachers and students disagree over how clean the classrooms and hallways should be. Business people and government officials disagree over how clean streets, waterways or parking lots should be. Everyone knows the definition of *clean*, of course, but very few people agree on how clean is clean enough in environmental disputes. Economists have their approach to cleanup issues, too. This lesson will provide an introduction to the economists' approach.

C. **Display Visual 5.1.** Read it with the students and discuss it briefly.

D. Ask the students to explain why one hiker had a problem with the heat while the other had no problem. After all, they both drank the same amount of water. The average and total consumption of water was exactly the same for each hiker. Assuming they are alike in every way except the manner in which they drank their water, what is the problem?

One should choose to drink water in a manner that enables the body to make good use of it. It is not the total amount of water that is important. What matters is drinking water when the body can best use it. We drink fluids on the margin; when we are a little bit thirsty, we drink a little bit of water. In that way, each additional drink comes when it will have the greatest additional benefit.

E. **Display Visual 5.2.** Go over the definitions presented. Ask the students to use the definitions to explain when the marginal benefits of drinking water became zero or less for hiker A.

Probably some time after bottle two or three, when the hiker no longer felt thirsty and his body felt full of water. From that point on, he received little or no benefit from the next six or seven bottles he drank.

F. To pursue the point, ask whether the total benefits hiker A received from drinking water would be equal to the total benefits hiker B received.

Hiker A's benefits would be less than those of hiker B. Hiker A received no benefits from bottles 4-10, while hiker B received benefits from each of the 10 bottles she drank.

G. What does all this have to do with environmental cleanup projects? Explain that the concept of marginal analysis also can be applied to analyzing the costs and benefits at stake in cleanup projects. **Distribute a copy of Activity 5.1** to each student. Read the Activity with the students and discuss it briefly. Then divide the class into groups of four or five students; assign the students to analyze the issue and recommend a correct policy. Each group should present its recommendations to the rest of the class.

H. After the students have completed their work on Activity 5.1, **distribute Activity 5.2.** Read the Activity with the students and discuss it briefly, emphasizing the proposed new focus on marginal analysis. Then assign the students, working again in their groups, to summarize what the consultants did.

Putting on their economists' hats, the consultants broke the total cost into marginal costs — that is, the cost of going from one level of cleanup to another level, measured in 10 percent increments. They did the same thing in analyzing benefits expected from the project.

I. Now turn to the consultants' new recommendation. Ask: Why would the consultants now recommend only a 70 percent cleanup of the lake when before they recommended an 80 percent cleanup?

After a 70 percent cleanup, cleaning the next 10 percent will cost an additional $20,000 and provide only $8,000 worth of additional benefits. To an economist, that would not be a wise choice — no more so than it would be wise to pay $20,000 for a car worth $8,000.

J. Turn to the other portion of the consultants' recommendation and consider it in light of the marginal analysis data. According to the data, what would be gained by spending the additional $20,000 on the Native Grass project?

The $20,000 expenditure would provide a 50 percent increase in native-grass area, valued at $150,000 of benefits. To an economist, this is a good deal!

K. What if additional money somehow became available? Ask: Would the consultants recommend spending enough additional money to increase the native-grass area to the 60 percent level?

Probably not, because it would cost an additional $15,000 to reach the 60 percent level, and that amount of additional spending would provide only an additional $8,000 worth of additional benefits. It would be better to find a different project where the additional funds would have a better use.

LESSON 5

CLOSURE

Ask the students to summarize the major points of this lesson.

1. Marginal cost is the additional cost of consuming an additional unit.

2. Marginal benefit is the additional benefit of consuming an additional unit.

3. Marginal analysis can help people make more careful decisions about environmental cleanup projects, using resources in such a way that the marginal benefits outweigh the marginal costs.

ASSESSMENT

Multiple-Choice Questions

1. Which of the following statements is most accurate?

   a. Average cost is the most useful measurement in economic reasoning.

   b. Total cost is the most useful measurement in economic reasoning.

   c. Marginal cost is the most useful measurement in economic reasoning.

   d. Comparing marginal costs and marginal benefits is the most useful measurement in economic reasoning.

2. Which of the following people would agree that a lake should be 100 percent clear of pollution?

   a. A person who plans to use the lake but will not have to incur any costs of cleaning the lake.

   b. A person who will not be using the lake and will have to pay most of the cleaning costs.

   c. Environmental engineers who must guarantee the lake is 100 percent pollution free or forfeit the fee for cleaning the lake.

   d. The public official in charge of the lake cleanup who is working with a small budget that will not be increased in the near future.

Essay Questions

1. Use your understanding of marginal analysis to respond to the following statement:

"Economic analysis is very superficial. Economists just compare the total cost of a project to the total benefits expected from the project. They call this cost/benefit analysis, but I call it just plain old common sense!"

The speaker is almost correct, but he or she does not understand the importance of marginal analysis. Marginal analysis measures the consequence of each additional change in the project. By comparing the marginal cost with the marginal benefits, economists can recommend stopping at a point where the marginal cost equals the marginal benefits. This is a less wasteful approach than seeking a point at which total costs equal total benefits.

2. In some controversial Superfund sites, officials have used the following standard to determine whether the site is cleaned well enough to place a school on the land that was previously polluted: "The soil must be clean enough that a child could eat small amounts of it daily for 254 days a year without significant harm." How would an economist respond to this standard? *(Hint: remember the clean lake/native grass projects you evaluated.)*

The economist would probably suggest that the standard is too stringent. If a child can run and play on the grounds without harmful effects, the soil would seem to be clean enough for health purposes. Cleaning it beyond that level would require high marginal costs and yield very few benefits. Most children do not eat soil 254 days per year. It seems unlikely that such a cleanup would be a wise use of environmental funds. A standard requiring that marginal costs must be close to the marginal benefits would free up resources for use on other more important environmental issues.

VISUAL 5.1

THE HYDRATION EXPERIMENT

Two hikers started their backpacking trip on the same hot day. They knew that they would be hiking for eight hours in 90-degree heat, so they each would need to drink at least 10 half-liter bottles of water.

Hiker A drank all 10 bottles of water at the beginning of the hike to "get it over with" and to "avoid carrying all that water on his back." Hiker A never made it to the destination.

Hiker B drank one bottle at the beginning of the hike; then she drank one bottle per hour during the rest of the hike, finishing the last bottle just as she arrived at her destination.

Both hikers were fit and healthy. Neither one had a sore ankle or any special burden to carry.

Explain why hiker B was successful while hiker A was not.

VISUAL 5.2

MARGINAL CONCEPTS

Marginal benefit: The additional benefit of consuming one more unit, such as one more bottle of water.

Total benefits: The sum of all the marginal benefits of consuming additional units, such as bottles of water.

Marginal cost: The additional cost of providing one more unit for consumption, such as the cost of one more bottle of water.

Total costs: The sum of all the marginal costs of consuming additional units, such as bottles of water.

ACTIVITY 5.1

THE PROBLEM OF THE DIRTY LAKE AND THE INVASIVE GRASS

Name_____

Imagine that you are members of Spanaway Lake Park Environmental Control Board. Your park suffers from two major problems: Lake pollution and invasive plant species.

The lake's pollution is caused by soil erosion, goose dung, yard debris, fertilizer runoff, litter and miscellaneous non-poisonous crud. If people swim in the lake, they get a skin rash from the polluted water.

The surrounding grassland suffers from many obnoxious weeds and invasive grasses that aggravate allergies and make it unpleasant for children to run and play in the park. Children who play in the park get small cuts from the sharp invasive grasses and pick up many "stickers" from the weeds. Native grasses are being forced out of the park by the invasive grasses and weeds.

The Control Board has received a $61,000 grant to pay for an environmental cleanup project. One group on the Board maintains that those funds should be used to clean up the lake. Another group wants to destroy the invasive grasses/weeds and plant native grasses in the park. To make the best decision, the Board has appointed a volunteer consulting group of environmental economists to assess the costs and benefits of each course of action. The group's initial findings are presented below. Study the findings and decide which project the Board should fund. Provide reasons for the decision.

A. The Clean-Lake Project

If $61,000 is spent on cleaning the lake, lake pollution levels will drop by 80 percent. The remaining 20 percent of pollution would then be hard to see with the human eye and it would have no negative impact on human health. Some species of fish would have trouble living in the lake, but most fish would thrive. The expected total benefits of this cleanup would be $336,000. This figure represents the value the clean lake would have for residents who use it and live and work nearby.

B. The Native-Grass Project

If $61,000 is spent on destroying invasive plants and replanting native grasses, 80 percent of the park could be reclaimed as native-grass areas. This change would reduce allergy problems and dramatically increase the amount of recreational space available in the park. The expected benefits of this cleanup would be $168,000. This figure represents the value the native-grass area would have for residents who use it and live and work nearby.

C. Related Information

The consulting group conducted a community poll to find out which project the community favored. Results showed that 50 percent of the people favored the Clean-Lake Project, 49 percent favored the Native-Grass Project, and 1 percent were undecided.

ACTIVITY 5.1, CONTINUED

The Board meets to make a decision based on this set of initial findings.
What should the Board decide?

_____

_____

What reasons might the Board give for its decision?

    1. _____

    2. _____

    3. _____

    4. _____

ACTIVITY 5.2

A MARGINAL ANALYSIS OF THE LAKE AND GRASS CLEANUP PROJECTS

Name_____

An Environmental Calculation

During the presentation of the Board's decision to the community, someone interrupts the speaker with this comment. "I thought these consultants were economists! How come they keep giving us total figures to base policy on? I took an econ class once and all the professor talked about was marginal analysis. Where is the marginal analysis here? Can't we find a decision that will let us use the money to help solve both problems?"

The consultants sheepishly explain that while arriving at their initial findings, they had suffered from a temporary "vapor lock of the brain." They promise to reanalyze the problem and come back with a marginal analysis of the cleanup project in time for the Board to consider at its next meeting. The Board agrees to postpone its decision until then. When the next meeting rolls around, the consultants provide the Board with a new analysis of the two cleanup projects. The new analysis is summarized below and on the next page.

A. The Native-Grass Project

N Grass Increase	Total Benefits	Marginal Benefits	Total Costs	Marginal Costs
0%	0	0	0	0
10%	$50,000	$50,000	$500	$500
20%	90,000	40,000	1,500	1,000
30%	120,000	30,000	3,000	1,500
40%	140,000	20,000	10,000	7,000
50%	150,000	10,000	20,000	10,000
60%	158,000	8,000	35,000	15,000
70%	164,000	6,000	42,000	17,000
80%	168,000	4,000	61,000	19,000
90%	170,000	2,000	83,000	22,000
100%	170,500	500	113,000	30,000

ACTIVITY 5.2, CONTINUED

B. The Clean-Lake Project

Pollution Reduction	Total Benefits	Marginal Benefits	Total Costs	Marginal Costs
0%	0	0	0	0
10%	$100,000	$100,000	$1,000	$1,000
20%	180,000	80,000	3,000	2,000
30%	240,000	60,000	6,000	3,000
40%	280,000	40,000	11,000	5,000
50%	300,000	20,000	19,000	8,000
60%	316,000	16,000	29,000	10,000
70%	328,000	12,000	41,000	12,000
80%	336,000	8,000	61,000	20,000
90%	340,000	4,000	86,000	25,000
100%	341,000	1000	116,000	30,000

C. Recommendations

The consultants recommend that $41,000 be spent on cleaning the lake; the remaining $20,000 should be used to reduce invasive grass and plant native grasses.

HOW CAN WE HELP
ENDANGERED SPECIES?

LESSON 6

HOW CAN WE HELP ENDANGERED SPECIES?

LESSON DESCRIPTION

The students are presented with information about the Endangered Species Act (ESA) and examples of species appearing on the protected list. They examine the history of species protection under the ESA. They are asked to imagine how the ESA would work if it were applied in the case of a dog living in their neighborhood. Finally, they assess the incentives created by the law and its enforcement procedures in order to decide whether the ESA helps or hinders efforts to protect endangered species.

BACKGROUND

According to the U.S. Fish and Wildlife Service, about 1,260 species of animals and plants are endangered or threatened with extinction in the United States. Examples include the American black bear, the piping plover, the loggerhead sea turtle, the West Indian manatee, the red-cockaded woodpecker and the sensitive joint-vetch. In order to protect such species and to increase their population numbers, the U.S. Congress enacted the Endangered Species Act (ESA) in 1973.

The ESA authorizes the U.S. Fish and Wildlife Service to establish a list of endangered species and requires citizens not to harm the listed species or their habitats. When an endangered species is found living on private land, the land owner is required to stop using that portion of land and leave it as habitat for the plant or animal. According to the ESA, the cost of protecting an endangered species is not to be considered in implementing the procedures deemed necessary to save it. And the costs must be borne by the landowner. Landowners are not compensated for losing the use of their land if it is taken out of production to provide habitat for an endangered species.

The ESA has been in effect for more than 30 years. There are two major categories for species classification, endangered or threatened. *Endangered* is the most severe classification. It means that the species numbers are declining rapidly and the species is very near extinction. *Threatened* is a less severe status indicating that the species' population numbers are very low but the species is not in immediate danger of extinction. Since the law's passage, 39 species have been delisted. Of those, 13 were delisted as a result of a population recovery. Others were delisted because of extinction, a taxonomic revision, or new information. Most of the recovered species were upgraded to a threatened status but still remain on the list of protected species. For information about delisting, see http://ecos.fws.gov/tess_public/TESSWebpageDelisted?listings=0.

Some evidence indicates that species habitat declines quickly after a species is listed as endangered by the Fish and Wildlife Service. For example, some forest owners may decide to harvest their trees sooner rather than later upon learning that an endangered species of bird might begin to nest in the trees when the trees mature.

EcoMYSTERY

How could it be that a law designed to protect endangered species might encourage people to destroy the habitat of endangered species?

ECONOMIC REASONING

By ruling out any consideration of the costs that arise from its enforcement, the ESA creates incentives that discourage people from protecting endangered species (EcoDetection principles 2 and 5). The key assumption underlying the ESA is that animals and plants provide a benefit to everybody. Since the public receives benefits from plants and animals, individual landowners should not be allowed to harm plants and animals that are endangered — even if protecting them requires landowners to hold back on farming, grazing, building or other activities that landowners ordinarily are free to pursue. As a result, the public receives a benefit that it does not pay for. The costs of protecting the endangered species are borne by individuals who live and work near the species' habitat.

Many landowners resent having to pay these costs for others, with no compensation, and many therefore attempt to avoid the costs (EcoDetection principle 2). One way to avoid the costs is to take action regarding land they own so that it will be unattractive to endangered species. Landowners might cut trees prematurely, for example, so that their trees do not become nesting places for endangered owls later on. If no endangered species take up residence on their land, the landowners can avoid the costs of protecting the species in question.

By concentrating costs on one small group without compensating them for losses they incur, the ESA creates an incentive that encourages people to try to keep endangered species off their property. This incentive is not conducive to nurturing endangered species. In the words of one economist, "it makes an innocent species an enemy to landowners."

ECONOMIC CONCEPTS

• Anticipated benefits

• Anticipated costs

• Incentives

OBJECTIVES

Students will:

1. Become familiar with endangered species listings for their state.

2. Examine a neighborhood situation in which a cocker spaniel is treated as an endangered species.

3. Use the concept of *incentives* to analyze people's reactions to the cocker spaniel once it is identified as an endangered species.

4. Use the concepts of *anticipated costs* and *anticipated benefits* to explain why endangered species habitat has declined.

CONTENT STANDARDS

• Productive resources are limited. Therefore, people cannot have all the goods and services they want; as a result, they must choose some things and give up others. (NCEE Content Standard 1.)

• People respond predictably to positive and negative incentives. (NCEE Content Standard 4.)

• Institutions evolve in market economies to help individuals and groups accomplish their goals. Banks, labor unions, corporations, legal systems, and not-for-profit organizations are examples of important institutions. A different kind of institution, clearly defined and well enforced property rights, is essential to a market economy. (NCEE Content Standard 10.)

• There is an economic role for government to play in a market economy whenever the benefits of a government policy outweigh its costs. Governments often provide for national defense, address environmental concerns, define and protect property rights, and attempt to make markets more competitive. Most government policies also redistribute income. (NCEE Content Standard 16.)

• Costs of government policies sometimes exceed benefits. This may occur because of incentives facing voters, government officials, and government employees, because of actions by special interest groups that can impose costs on the general public, or because social goals other than economic efficiency are being pursued. (NCEE Content Standard 17.)

TIME

60 minutes

MATERIALS

• A transparency of Visuals 6.1, 6.2, 6.3, 6.4, 6.5 and 6.6

• A copy of Activities 6.1 and 6.2 for each student

PROCEDURE

A. Explain that the purpose of this lesson is to demonstrate how efforts to protect endangered species can unintentionally put endangered species at risk.

B. **Display Visual 6.1.** Explain that the bald eagle it depicts nearly became extinct in the lower 48 states of the United States. To protect the bald eagle and other endangered species, Congress in 1973 passed the Endangered Species Act (ESA).

C. **Display Visual 6.2.** Note that the number of species on the endangered species list has grown to 1,263 plants and animals.

D. **Distribute a copy of Activity 6.1** to each student and **display Visual 6.3.** (For more information, the students may visit http://ecos.fws.gov/tess.) Ask:

1. What do you notice about the distribution of endangered species across the different states?

   Some states have more endangered species than others.

2. Which state has the least endangered species?

   Alaska, with six.

3. Which state has the most endangered species?

   Hawaii, with 312.

4. How many endangered species are listed for your state?

LESSON 6

E. Explain a key problem associated with federal protection under the ESA. The purpose of the law is to identify, protect and restore endangered species to healthy numbers so that they can be removed from the list. (For background information, teachers may wish to read the Endangered Species Act and its Implementation Guidelines. The ESA can be found at http://endangered.fws.gov/esaall.pdf and the Implementation Guidelines can be found at http://access.gpo.gov/nara/cfr/waisidx 02/50cfr17 02.html. The Act is about 40 pages long, and the guidelines are well over 100 pages.) In practice, however, only about 39 species have been changed to a threatened status or removed from the list. Of those, only 13 have been changed (delisted) because of an increase in their population numbers. Seven have become extinct and the rest have been removed as a result of new information or because of a taxonomic revision.

F. **Display Visual 6.4** and briefly discuss the mystery it poses: How could a law designed to protect endangered species encourage people to destroy the habitat of endangered species? Tell the students to get out their copy of the principles of EcoDetection. They will make use of these principles as they work to solve the mystery.

G. To begin the analysis, emphasize a preliminary problem. It is difficult to observe and analyze endangered species directly. Very few of us live near them. But we can make a start by considering an analogy. We can focus on something very familiar to us and see how the law might influence us if it were applied to that familiar item.

H. **Display Visual 6.5**, revealing only the title and the illustration.

I. Explain that cocker spaniels are very popular dogs — not too big, friendly, smart, easy to train. What would happen if someone in your neighborhood had such a dog?

Most people would like the dog. They would enjoy seeing it play. They probably would want to pet it and throw sticks for it to fetch.

J. Tell the students now to stretch their imaginations. They should assume that their community has passed a new cocker-spaniel protection law — one with provisions such as the following.

Here, reveal the rest of the content of **Visual 6.5** and allow a moment for the students to read it.

What effect might this law have on people's attitudes toward cocker spaniels?

As necessary, help the students to grasp the potential consequences of this law. The anticipated costs have changed. Now you can't park your car in your driveway if the cocker spaniel likes to sun herself on the driveway's warm asphalt; you can't change the landscaping around your house if the cocker spaniel enjoys using the landscaping as it is; if you have a couch that the cocker spaniel likes to jump up on, you can't get rid of the couch unless your action is approved by the community's cocker-spaniel protection monitors, etc. As a result of such consequences, many people in the neighborhood might begin to feel unfriendly to the cocker spaniel.

K. To be more precise about the reasons for this change in attitudes, ask the students to explain the change by reference to principles of EcoDetection.

EcoDetection principles 2, 3, 4 and 5 apply directly. Under the new law, the incentives have changed. The dog is no longer a lovable pet. She is now a problem. She imposes new costs on the neighbors without providing any new benefits. They therefore have no incentive to make the dog feel welcome. Far from it. They would be happy to see her gone. Thus the dog's owner may feel pressure to keep the dog at home. Depending on how steep the neighbors' costs turn out to be, the dog may even be at risk of disappearing from the neighborhood — a victim of foul play.

L. Ask: What caused the innocent dog to become an unpleasant, unwelcome intruder? Did the dog change?

No. The rules changed, imposing new costs, for which neighbors would not be compensated, and creating no new benefits. Even before the new costs actually materialize, the new rule is a problem because people have begun to anticipate how they will be affected by it.

M. **Display Visual 6.6.** (*It lists endangered species in Louisiana. You may prefer to use the list for your state; you can find that list at the Fish and Wildlife Service Web site.*) Ask: Would a red-cockaded woodpecker be a welcome visitor to timber land owned by a person who needs to harvest mature trees to earn income?

Probably not. Red-cockaded woodpeckers like to live in old trees. Timber owners like to cut trees when they are mature, and then grow new ones. That is how they earn their living. Red-cockaded woodpeckers would be unwelcome guests if their presence meant that a landowner could not cut his or her mature trees.

N. **Distribute Activity 6.2.** Ask the students to respond to the Questions for Discussion.

1. Which statements identify incentives that would encourage Johnny to be a good steward of woodpecker habitat?

   Statements a and e.

2. Which statements identify incentives that would discourage Johnny from being a good steward of woodpecker habitat?

   Statements b, c, d, f, g and h.

3. What do you think Johnny will do about the woodpeckers?

   To avoid problems with the U.S. Fish and Wildlife Service, he will probably protect the colony currently living in his trees and begin to cut all the other trees so that no new woodpecker colonies settle in his forest.

CLOSURE

Summarize the main point of the lesson, using the principles of EcoDetection. How could it be that a law intended to protect endangered species unintentionally put certain species and their habitat at greater risk?

If the law imposes too high a cost on landowners without helping them to pay those costs, some will alter the habitat in an effort to avoid paying. If the habitat becomes unsuitable for use by the endangered species, the landowners will not have to bear the costs of species protection.

ASSESSMENT

Multiple-Choice Questions

1. Which of the following statements is most accurate?

   a. Only evil people would harm an endangered species.

   b. People will help protect endangered species no matter what the efforts cost them.

   c. People will not help endangered species unless the government forces them to do so.

   d. High costs will discourage people from protecting endangered species.

2. Which of the following plans would help to preserve the red-cockaded woodpecker habitat in private forests?

   a. Require owners of the forest to feed the woodpeckers three times per day.

   b. Ask all bird watchers to make room for woodpecker nests in their homes.

   c. Require forest owners to leave 80 acres of trees undisturbed around each woodpecker nest.

   d. Stop collecting property taxes for land used by the woodpeckers.

Essay Questions

1. Respond to this argument:

   "Landowners object to protecting endangered species on their properties. They say it costs too much to provide the protection required. But their argument is unfounded. The law does not require landowners to spend any money. They just have to leave the habitat as it exists."

   The cost landowners incur is an opportunity cost. They are prevented from using their land for purposes that will produce income. The lost opportunity to gain income is a cost just as important as paying money out of one's bank account.

2. Respond to this suggestion, using one or more principles of EcoDetection to support your answer.

   "The effort to save endangered species could be more successful if landowners were paid a generous amount of income to increase endangered species populations on their land."

   This point is consistent with EcoDetection principles 2 and 5. Landowners incur costs, usually in the form of lost income, when protecting endangered species. If the rules were changed to provide landowners with income to cover their costs, they would have a stronger incentive to protect and nurture endangered species.

LESSON 6

VISUAL 6.1

THE BALD EAGLE

VISUAL 6.2

THREATENED OR ENDANGERED SPECIES

Species Listed as Threatened or Endangered in the United States (May 2003)

- Total species: 1,263
  (517 animals, 746 plants)

- Total species threatened
  (low numbers but not on the verge of extinction): 276
  (129 animals, 147 plants)

- Total species endangered
  (numbers so low they are on the verge of extinction): 987
  (388 animals, 599 plants)

Source: U.S. Fish and Wildlife Service

Visual 6.3

United States Map of Endangered Species

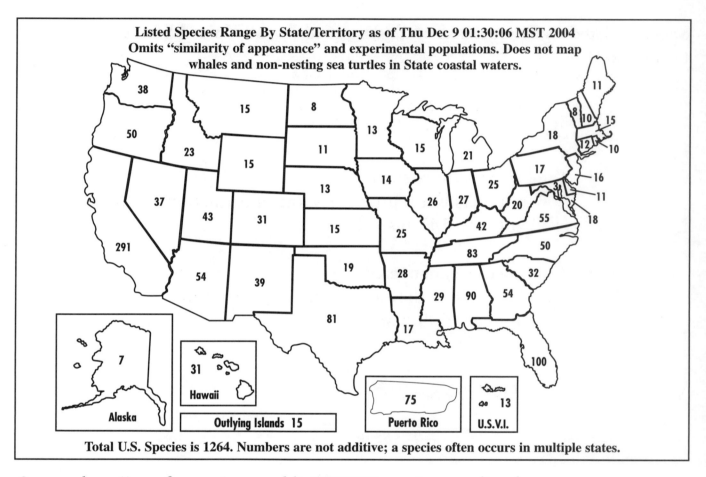

Listed Species Range By State/Territory as of Thu Dec 9 01:30:06 MST 2004
Omits "similarity of appearance" and experimental populations. Does not map whales and non-nesting sea turtles in State coastal waters.

Total U.S. Species is 1264. Numbers are not additive; a species often occurs in multiple states.

Source: http://ecos.fws.gov/tess_public/TESSUsmap?status=listed

VISUAL 6.4

THE ENDANGERED SPECIES MYSTERY

How could it be that a law designed to protect endangered species would encourage people to destroy the habitat of endangered species?

VISUAL 6.5

WOULD WE STILL LOVE COCKER SPANIELS IF THEY WERE ENDANGERED?

A new law states, "Anywhere a cocker spaniel is known to be living, the area must be preserved. No changes can be made in that environment, and any humans living in the area must not disturb the dog. Anyone living near a cocker spaniel must report it to authorities so the area can be monitored for cocker-spaniel protection. This law will be enforced without regard for objections arising from the costs its enforcement may impose on residents, and no compensation will be awarded for any claims of cost."

VISUAL 6.6

THREATENED AND ENDANGERED SPECIES OF LOUISIANA (26)

ANIMALS (23)

Status	Listing
T	Alligator, American
T	Bear, American black
T	Bear, Louisiana black
T	Eagle, bald
T	Heelsplitter, Alabama
E	Mucket, pink
T	Pearlshell, Louisiana
E	Pelican, brown
T	Plover, piping
T	Sea turtle, green
E	Sea turtle, hawksbill
E	Sea turtle, leatherback
T	Sea turtle, loggerhead
T	Sturgeon, gulf
E	Sturgeon, pallid
E	Tern, least
T	Tortoise, gopher
T	Turtle, ringed map
E	Vireo, black-capped
E	Whale, finback
E	Whale, humpback
E	Woodpecker, red-cockaded

PLANTS (3)

Status	Listing
T	Geocarpon minimum
E	Quillwort, Louisiana
E	Chaffseed, American

Source: http://endangered.fws.gov

Activity 6.1

Map of Endangered Species Listed by State

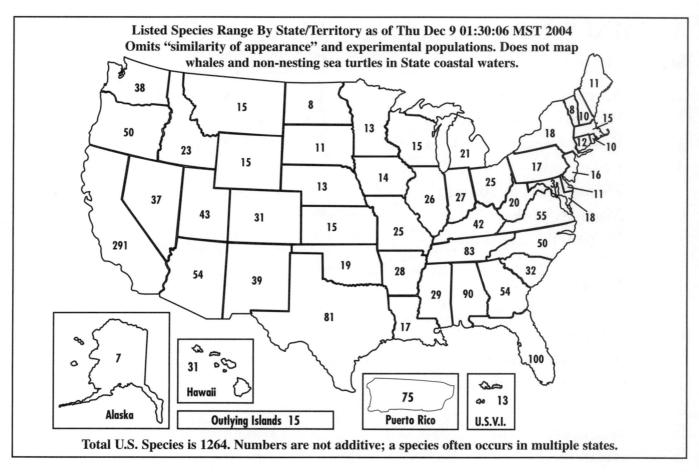

Listed Species Range By State/Territory as of Thu Dec 9 01:30:06 MST 2004
Omits "similarity of appearance" and experimental populations. Does not map whales and non-nesting sea turtles in State coastal waters.

Total U.S. Species is 1264. Numbers are not additive; a species often occurs in multiple states.

Source: http://ecos.fws.gov/tess_public/TESSUsmap?status=listed

ACTIVITY 6.2

INCENTIVES AND ENDANGERED SPECIES PROTECTION

Name_____

A red-cockaded woodpecker colony has come to live in the privately owned timber land of Johnny Appleseed. Johnny has always tried to be a good steward of his land and forests. He has trees of diverse ages and species in the forest. He selectively logs his trees to minimize the erosion caused by harvesting lumber. In the past, he cut his trees on an 80-year rotation instead of the 40-year rotation practiced by other timber owners. Now Johnny has learned that red-cockaded woodpeckers like to live in trees 60 years old and older.

Questions for Discussion

1. Which of the following statements identify incentives that would encourage Johnny to be a good steward of woodpecker habitat?

2. Which of the following statements identify incentives that would discourage Johnny from being a good steward of woodpecker habitat?

3. What do you think Johnny will do about the woodpeckers?

The Statements

a. He feels a responsibility to protect endangered species.

b. He knows that other colonies of red-cockaded woodpeckers live in Louisiana. His property is not their only habitat.

c. He will be fined $100,000 and sentenced to serve up to five years in jail if he harms the woodpeckers or their habitat.

d. He will lose about $100,000 if he cannot harvest his old trees.

e. Environmental advocates will praise him for caring for the woodpeckers.

f. Most of his trees are between 40 and 60 years old. If he harvests these trees he will receive about 90 percent of the income he would receive for 80-year-old trees.

g. If red-cockaded woodpeckers nest in his forest, he will receive regular visits from individuals working for the U.S Fish and Wildlife Service to monitor his treatment of the woodpeckers.

h. Under the law he is allowed to harvest trees that are 60 years old and younger.

CAN INCENTIVES PROTECT ENDANGERED SPECIES?

LESSON 7

CAN INCENTIVES PROTECT ENDANGERED SPECIES?

LESSON DESCRIPTION

The students discuss ways to protect fish placed on display in a science class. By viewing visuals, they learn about key provisions of the Endangered Species Act. They role-play international commissioners and make recommendations regarding policies to protect endangered species.

BACKGROUND

Among animal species that have declined nearly to the point of extinction, some have been highly valued. The buffalo were valued by American Indians and white hunters in the nineteenth century. American Indians used parts of the buffalo for shelter, clothing and food. They exchanged buffalo products with one another and with whites. Similarly, whites exchanged money for buffalo meat and used the meat to feed crews building the railroads. Today African elephants are valued for similar reasons. Ivory from elephant tusks is made into piano keys and carved into chess pieces. Elephants' hides are nearly as valuable; they can be made into boots and wallets.

ECOMYSTERY

American Indians and whites depended on the buffalo for food and clothing, much as people in North America depend on beef cattle today. Yet the buffalo nearly became extinct. By 1889, only about 150 were left. Today, however, the buffalo are back. Why?

Will the African elephant go the way of the American buffalo? Illegal hunters kill many elephants in several African nations, and the elephant population is declining. In southern Africa, however, the situation is different. The elephant populations of Zimbabwe, Botswana, Namibia and South Africa are increasing. Why?

ECONOMIC REASONING

Rewards for killing buffalo were high, while the rewards for protecting them were low and uncertain (EcoDetection principle 4). Nobody owned the buffalo, and it would have been difficult to establish rules of ownership or fence buffalo in even if ownership could have been established. Since nobody owned the

buffalo, nobody had anything to gain by trying to limit the killing (EcoDetection principle 6). A buffalo not taken today would be one that someone else took tomorrow. Today, however, private ownership is easily established, and many people own herds of buffalo (EcoDetection principle 5). Many shoppers buy buffalo meat, valuing it as an alternative to beef. People who own buffalo protect their herds and increase the size of their herds so they can sell buffalo as a food product (EcoDetection principle 6).

In Africa there has been a similar development. People tried at first to protect elephants by outlawing elephant hunting and by banning the sale of ivory (EcoDetection principle 5). But these bans drove up the price for ivory. Higher prices caused risk takers in some nations to decide that the rewards for taking elephants illegally were well worth the costs (EcoDetection principle 4). Thus, much killing continues. But in southern Africa some nations have tried an incentive approach to preserving the elephant. South Africa, for example, allows safari hunting (gun and photography) and tourism on private and state land for a fee. It also allows the legal sale of ivory and hides within the country. As a result, if South Africans protect the elephant population, they can sell hunting rights, ivory and hides — and benefit from the sales. Thus they have an incentive to protect elephants (EcoDetection principles 4 and 6).

ECONOMIC CONCEPTS

- Incentives
- Private property rights

OBJECTIVES

Students will:

1. Identify key provisions of the Endangered Species Act.

2. Analyze policy options for protecting endangered species, using the concept of *incentives* to predict which policies will be effective.

CONTENT STANDARDS

- People respond predictably to positive and negative incentives. (NCEE Content Standard 4.)

- Institutions evolve in market economies to help individuals and groups accomplish their goals. Banks, labor unions, corporations, legal systems, and not-for-profit organizations are examples of important institutions. A different kind of institution, clearly defined and well enforced property rights, is essential to a market economy. (NCEE Content Standard 10.)

- Investment in factories, machinery, new technology, and the health, education, and training of people can raise future standards of living. (NCEE Content Standard 15.)

TIME

75 minutes

MATERIALS

- A transparency of Visuals 7.1, 7.2, 7.3 and 7.4
- A copy of Activities 7.1 and 7.2 for each student

PROCEDURE

A. Explain the purpose of this lesson: The students will analyze protection of the environment, focusing on how rewards can be used to protect endangered species.

B. Explain that while all of us want to protect animals, it is not always clear how best to achieve this goal. Imagine a situation where the animals in a class aquarium need to be protected and cared for. How might it be best to do this?

C. **Display Visual 7.1.** Ask:

1. If Alternative 1 is followed, what incentives do members of the student council have to protect the aquarium and the fish?

    The student council members will have little incentive to protect the aquarium or the fish. The council would need to depend on the good will of an interested member or two.

2. Do you think Alternative 1 is likely to be a success?

    Probably not. The student council has a weak interest in the outcome.

3. If Alternative 2 is followed, what are the incentives for Jeremy to protect the aquarium and the fish?

    Jeremy is the owner of the aquarium and the fish. He wants the aquarium and the fish to be returned to him in good condition. He would have

a strong incentive to devise a plan that would ensure protection for the aquarium and the fish.

4. Do you think Alternative 2 is likely to be a success?

    Probably. Jeremy has a strong interest in the outcome.

D. Explain that the rewards involved in taking care of Jeremy's aquarium and fish are similar to the rewards involved in protecting endangered species. While all of us want to preserve endangered species, it is not always clear how best to achieve this goal. Some environmental policies involve high costs and uncertain benefits.

E. **Display Visual 7.2.** Explain the basic provisions of the Endangered Species Act (ESA). Note that the rules of the ESA regarding endangered species are simple. It is illegal to do anything that threatens a member of an endangered species.

F. **Display Visual 7.3.** Ask the class to note that there are more than 1,000 animal and plant species on the list. More than 500 animals and nearly 800 plants are listed as endangered or threatened by the U.S. government. Explain that an "endangered" species is one that is in danger of extinction throughout all or a significant portion of its range. A "threatened" species is one that is likely to become endangered in the foreseeable future.

G. Point out that sometimes the rules set by the ESA have unanticipated consequences. Some unanticipated consequences can harm rather than help endangered species. **Display Visual 7.4.** Invite the students to speculate on why elephants might be shot illegally or why a rancher would protect a family of wolves.

H. **Distribute Activity 7.1.** Ask the students to read the Activity and prepare answers to the discussion questions. Discuss the questions and the students' responses.

Questions for Discussion: The Buffalo

1. Why did American Indians and whites hunt the buffalo?

    American Indians used parts of the buffalo for shelter, clothing and food. Whites used buffalo meat to feed crews building the railroads. Buffalo hides became popular for making robes.

LESSON 7

2. Why did the buffalo nearly become extinct?

Nobody owned the buffalo. Nobody would have benefited by trying to preserve the buffalo. Buffalo not taken by one hunter today would be taken by someone else tomorrow.

3. Why are the buffalo back?

Most buffalo today are privately owned. Herds are being increased in order to produce meat desired by consumers.

Questions for Discussion: The Elephants

1. Why are elephants not loved by everybody? Who could hate elephants?

African elephants are valued by hunters because of their tusks and hides. Farmers don't value elephants because elephants can destroy crops. Americans who have trouble understanding this should take note of how suburban residents react when deer eat everything in their gardens.

2. Why have bans on the sale of ivory failed to protect elephant populations?

The bans on hunting and importing have increased the price for ivory. The high prices have attracted poachers who are willing to take high risks.

3. What policies have some nations in southern Africa tried?

South Africa allows safari hunting for a fee. It also allows the legal sale of ivory and hides within the country. The Zimbabwe Department of National Parks and Wildlife Management gives local farmers permission to hunt some elephants and other game. The hunters benefit by gaining meat and hides. The fees paid by the hunters help to support wildlife management services; they also provide income for families and help to pay for schools and other public goods.

4. Why have these policies been more successful?

The fees from legal sales of hunting rights, and the money people can make by harvesting game, are rewards to local citizens. These rewards give local citizens an interest in preserving the herds of game and keeping poachers out.

I. **Distribute Activity 7.2.** Divide the class into small groups. In each group, the students should discuss the questions and prepare policy recommendations.

CASE 1
Saving the Wolves: Policy Choice A

1. What are the costs to ranchers?

They can not use their land in the way they would like to.

2. What are the costs to other tax-paying citizens?

Very few — the costs are borne by the ranchers.

3. What are the benefits to ranchers?

Ranchers who wish to reintroduce wolves will feel good about protecting wolves. Other ranchers will not benefit.

4. Will the ranchers protect the wolves?

Given the high costs and limited benefits, probably not.

CASE 1
Saving the Wolves: Policy Choice B

1. What are the costs to ranchers?

They cannot use their land in the way they would like to.

2. What are the benefits to ranchers?

They are compensated for the wolves' use of their land.

3. What are the costs to other tax-paying citizens?

Taxpayers would pay for the compensation ranchers receive for letting wolves use their land.

4. Will the ranchers voluntarily protect the wolves?

Since the benefits are more advantageous in this option, many ranchers will voluntarily comply.

CASE 2
Saving the Owls: Policy Choice A

1. What are the costs to forest owners?

They cannot use their forest land in the way they would like to.

2. What are the costs to other tax-paying citizens?

Very few — the costs are borne by the forest owners.

3. What are the benefits to forest owners?

Forest owners who wish to preserve owls will feel good.

4. Will the forest owners protect owls?

Given the high costs and limited benefits, probably not.

CASE 2
Saving the Owls: Policy Choice B

1. What are the costs to forest owners?

   They cannot use their forest land in the way they would like to.

2. What are the benefits to forest owners?

   They are compensated for the owls' use of the land.

3. What are the costs to other tax-paying citizens?

   Taxpayers would pay for the compensation forest owners receive for letting owls use their land.

4. Will the forest owners protect the owls?

   Since the benefits are more advantageous in this option, many forest owners will voluntarily comply.

CLOSURE

Review key points of the lesson. Ask: Which policies are more likely to gain widespread cooperation in the effort to protect endangered species?

Policies that reward voluntary compliance by providing benefits for the public use of private resources.

Display Visual 7.4 again and invite the students to solve the mysteries:

- Why would poachers kill elephants when the government says not to?

  People are willing to pay for elephant tusks and hides. Also, elephants destroy crops. Thus, people can benefit by killing elephants. The bans on hunting elephants and importing tusks and hides do little to reward people for looking after elephants. They only encourage risk takers to kill all the elephants they can find.

- Why would some ranchers protect wolves when wolves are predators that sometimes kill sheep and cattle?

  Some private organizations such as the Defenders of Wildlife are willing to compensate ranchers who allow wolves to remain on their land.

ASSESSMENT

Multiple-Choice Questions

1. Why are elephant populations increasing in southern Africa?

   a. Passage of South Africa's Endangered Species Act

   b. New vaccines to prevent disease

   c. Poor nutrition

   d. Policies allowing local people to benefit from the elephant

2. Which of the following is not a feature of the Endangered Species Act?

   a. The ESA provides for identifying endangered species.

   b. To "take" an endangered species means to harm, harass, pursue, hunt, shoot, wound, kill and so forth.

   c. Protection of an endangered species is limited only to the geographical area where the species lives.

   d. The ESA is administered primarily by the U.S. Fish and Wildlife Service.

Essay Question

Wetlands are critical to the survival of migrating birds. For example, ducks need places to stop along their migration routes from South America to North America. Yet farmers and land developers often do not wish to preserve wetlands because wetlands preservation reduces their incomes. What are the costs of wetlands protection to the owners? What are the benefits? Will property owners voluntarily protect the wetlands? How could incentives be used to encourage farmers and land developers to protect wetlands?

The cost to the farmers and developers is the income they will not earn if they protect the wetlands. The benefit to farmers and developers is that they may feel good if they protect the wetlands. Given that the costs are high and the benefits are low and uncertain, many landowners will not protect the wetlands voluntarily. However, if some incentive were provided — such as a payment for preserving the wetlands — land owners would be more willing to cooperate. The payment might come from a private organization such as Ducks Unlimited.

VISUAL 7.1

FISH GO TO SCHOOL

Mr. Wizard teaches biology. He wants to obtain an aquarium that can display local species of fish for his students to study.

Jeremy is a student in Mr. Wizard's class. He is very interested in fish. He wants to provide an aquarium complete with two smallmouth bass. He would like the aquarium and the two bass to be returned to him at the end of the school year.

Mr. Wizard must choose how best to care for the aquarium and its inhabitants. His students have proposed two alternatives:

ALTERNATIVE 1

School policy is unclear about allowing students to have their property used by others, even for educational purposes. Some students say that if the school is to use the aquarium, it must be owned by the school. They suggest that the student council should take over ownership of the aquarium and the fish. The student council would have responsibility to protect the aquarium and the fish. It would return the aquarium to Jeremy at the end of the year.

ALTERNATIVE 2

Other students think that the Jeremy is only lending the aquarium and the fish to the science classes. It would be best if he maintained ownership and held full responsibility for seeing to it that the aquarium and its inhabitants will be protected.

VISUAL 7.1, CONTINUED

Questions for Discussion

1. If Alternative 1 is followed, what incentives do members of the student council have to protect the aquarium and the fish?

2. Do you think that Alternative 1 is likely to be a success?

3. If Alternative 2 is followed, what are the incentives for Jeremy to protect the aquarium and the fish?

4. Do you think that Alternative 2 is likely to be a success?

Visual 7.2

Key Provisions of the Endangered Species Act

- It was passed originally in 1973.

- It is administered by the U.S. Fish and Wildlife Service.

- It lists endangered species.

- It identifies "critical habitat" for listed species. Critical habitat includes geographic areas on which features are found that are thought to be critical for the species to survive. Critical habitat may include areas not occupied by the species.

- It outlaws the "taking" of a listed species. The Act says, "The term *take* means to harass, harm pursue, hunt, shoot, wound, kill, trap, capture, or collect or attempt to engage in any such conduct."

VISUAL 7.3

THREATENED AND ENDANGERED ANIMALS AND PLANTS LISTED BY THE U.S. FISH & WILDLIFE SERVICE

Group	Endangered	Threatened
Mammals	69	9
Birds	77	14
Reptiles	14	22
Amphibians	12	9
Fishes	71	43
Clams	62	8
Snails	21	11
Insects	35	9
Arachnids	12	0
Crustaceans	18	3
Animal Sub Total	**391**	**128**
Flowering plants	571	144
Conifers and cycads	2	1
Ferns	24	2
Lichens	2	0
Plant sub total	599	147
Grand total	**990**	**275**

VISUAL 7.4

TWO ECOMYSTERIES

THE ELEGANT ELEPHANTS MYSTERY

Elephants are elegant animals. They are an important element of the environment of Africa and are protected by national and international laws that ban the sale of ivory. But some people continue to kill elephants. Why would people kill elephants when the government says not to?

THE WONDERFUL WOLVES MYSTERY

Wolves are wonderful animals. They were an important element of the environment in early North American woodlands and in the West. But wolves are predators; they sometimes kill livestock owned by ranchers and farmers. Moreover, the government is not willing to compensate ranchers for any livestock lost to wolves. Yet some Montana ranchers protect wolves — known predators that may kill livestock. Why?

ACTIVITY 7.1

INTERNATIONAL SPECIES PROTECTION COMMISSION

Name_____

You have been appointed to serve on the International Species Protection Commission. The purpose of the commission is to give advice to national leaders on how best to preserve endangered species.

The commission has often been praised for its clear analysis of problems. The success of past commission efforts can be explained by the fact that it follows the principles of EcoDetection when examining policy recommendations:

1. Resources are scarce; therefore, people must choose.

2. People's choices involve cost.

3. People's choices influence environmental quality.

4. People's choices are influenced by incentives.

5. People create rules that influence choices and incentives.

6. People take better care of things they own and value.

Resources are scarce; this requires people to make choices, even with regard to the environment. People's voluntary choices can improve the environment. But because all choices involve costs, people need rewards to encourage them to act in ways that will protect the environment. If people can benefit from protecting endangered species, then they will be willing stewards of the environment. If people are punished for the uses they make of their property, they may respond in ways we would not expect, and these responses might be harmful to the environment. The rewards in question can be provided by laws (rules) passed by governments.

YOUR JOB

Read and discuss the case studies prepared by your staff on the buffalo and the elephant. Answer the Questions for Discussion. In Activity 7.2, you will be asked to do a similar analysis.

The Demise and Rise of the Buffalo

The buffalo offered a lot to American Indians and white hunters. North American Indians used parts of the buffalo for shelter, clothing and food. They also exchanged buffalo products with one another and with whites. Similarly, whites exchanged money for buffalo meat that they used to feed crews building the railroads. And buffalo hide became a popular material for making robes.

The buffalo were big, strong, tough animals. Many thousands of them migrated across the plains from one Indian hunting territory to another. Unable to restrict these wanderers and thus establish ownership, Indians had little to gain from preserving them. If a hunter from one group did not shoot a buffalo, one from another group might. Moreover, the other hunters might be enemies. No rewards encouraged Indians to preserve the buffalo. Whites faced a similar situation. Rewards for taking the buffalo were high. Buffalo provided a cheap source of food for crews building the railroads, and they provided popular material for clothing. But it would have been difficult to establish ownership rules for buffalo. It was too expensive to fence in the herds, and nobody could determine who owned free-range buffalo. Since no one owned the buffalo, nobody would benefit by limiting the killing. A buffalo not taken today would be one that someone else took tomorrow. As a result, the buffalo nearly became extinct. By 1889, only about 150 buffalo had survived.

Activity 7.1, Continued

Today, however, the buffalo are back. Property rights for the buffalo now are clearly defined. Most buffalo now are raised on private ranches. They no longer roam the prairies and plains, unclaimed. As a result, the buffalo population is rebounding. Privately owned buffalo today number at least 130,000. Private owners of buffalo are building up herds in order to produce meat desired by consumers. Some consumers like buffalo meat because it is relatively low in calories, cholesterol and fat.

Questions for Discussion: The Buffalo

1. Why did North American Indians and whites hunt the buffalo?

2. Why did the buffalo nearly become extinct?

3. Why are the buffalo back?

How to Help the Elephants

African elephants are valued because of their tusks. Ivory from the tusks is made into piano keys and chess pieces. Elephants' hides are also valuable. Hides can be made into boots and wallets. Apart from these considerations, not everybody loves elephants. Elephants are not good neighbors. Poor African farmers, for example, do not welcome elephants who stomp on their crops.

Because elephants are valued for their ivory and hide and hated for the damage they do to crops, it is not a surprise that they are being hunted into near-extinction in parts of Africa. What should be done? In an effort to reduce the ivory trade and protect the elephants, Kenya has banned the hunting of elephants. And many nations ban the import of ivory.

What has the result of these actions been? Unfortunately for the elephant, the populations have continued to decline. Why? Illegal hunters — poachers — have stepped up their activities. The bans on hunting and importing have increased the price for ivory. The chance to make a great deal of money in the illegal ivory trade has attracted risk takers — people willing to risk being arrested or shot in return for the chance to make a great deal of money. These hunters have little reason to worry about preserving the elephant population. An elephant that gets away is just one that some other poacher might kill.

In southern Africa, the situation is different. The elephant populations of Zimbabwe, Botswana, Namibia and South Africa are increasing. Governments in these countries have followed different polices. South Africa, for example, allows safari hunting (gun and photography) and tourism on private and state land for a fee. Until an international treaty banned trade in ivory, South Africa also allowed the legal sale of ivory and hides. The sale of hunting rights and animal products gives South Africans a reward for looking after elephants.

Zimbabwe has followed similar polices. For example, the Zimbabwe Department of National Parks and Wildlife Management gives local farmers permission to hunt a certain number of elephants and some other game. The local farmers can hunt the animals themselves or sell the hunting permits to commercial hunters. The profits generated by these activities reward local farmers for preserving the animals and keeping poachers out.

ACTIVITY 7.1, CONTINUED

Questions for Discussion: The Elephants

1. Why are elephants loved? Hated?

2. Why have bans on the sale and importation of ivory failed to protect elephant populations?

3. How have the nations in southern Africa tried to protect elephants?

4. Why have these policies been more successful?

LESSON 7

ACTIVITY 7.2

POLICY ANALYSIS

Name_____

The International Species Protection Commission uses the principles of EcoDetection to guide it in recommending actions to be taken by governments. Review the principles below. Then read the following two cases, discuss the questions, and make your recommendations.

The commission has often been praised by environmental groups for its clear analysis of problems. The success of past commission efforts can be explained by the fact that it follows these principles of EcoDetection when examining policy recommendations:

1. Resources are scarce; therefore, people must choose.
2. People's choices involve cost.
3. People's choices influence environmental quality.
4. People's choices are influenced by incentives.
5. People create rules that influence choices and incentives.
6. People take better care of things they own and value.

CASE 1 SAVING THE WOLVES

Policy Goal Wolves once lived in many places in North America. They were hunted and trapped into near extinction. Environmentalists wish to reintroduce wolves to the western United States. Today wolves would help to balance the ecology. In Montana, for example, wolves would help control the populations of deer and elk, which now over-graze the land.

Policy Choice A

When wolves are discovered on private property, require ranchers to protect the wolves. For example, ranchers should not come close to the wolves or harm them in any way.

1. What are the costs to ranchers?

2. What are the costs to other tax-paying citizens?

3. What are the benefits to ranchers?

4. Will the ranchers protect the wolves?

ACTIVITY 7.2, CONTINUED

Policy Choice B

When wolves are discovered on private property, pay the rancher $5,000 for not using the land occupied by the wolves and for any risk the wolves present to the ranchers' livestock.

1. What are the costs to ranchers?

2. What are the benefits to ranchers?

3. What are the costs to other tax-paying citizens?

4. Will the ranchers voluntarily protect the wolves?

Policy Recommendation: Which policy do you favor (A or B)? Why?

CASE 2 SAVING THE OWLS

Policy Goal: Government biologists have discovered a rare owl that lives in certain trees in the western United States. The government would like to protect this owl species.

Policy Choice A

When owls are discovered on privately owned forest land, require the owner to protect the owl. For example, the land owner may not harvest any trees within 20 miles of the owls' nests or harm the owls in any way.

1. What are the costs to the forest owners?

2. What are the costs to other tax-paying citizens?

3. What are the benefits to the forest owners?

4. Will the forest owners protect owls?

ACTIVITY 7.2, CONTINUED

Policy Choice B

When owls are discovered on privately owned forest land, pay the landowner for not using the land around the nests. For example, pay the owner $5,000 at the end of each year when a nest on the land has been successfully preserved.

1. What are the costs to the forest owners?

2. What are the benefits to the forest owners?

3. What are the costs to other tax-paying citizens?

4. Will the forest owners protect the owls?

Policy Recommendation: Which policy do you favor (A or B)? Why?

THE COSTS AND BENEFITS OF HAVING CHILDREN

LESSON 8

THE COSTS AND BENEFITS OF HAVING CHILDREN

LESSON DESCRIPTION

The students analyze data about rich and poor countries in order to examine the impact of economic wealth on population growth. Then they read a letter written by a Wisconsin farmer in 1854 regarding the work done by children in his household. They compare the value that children bring to a household in poor countries today with the value the children brought to the Wisconsin farm in 1854. Finally, they draw conclusions about the impact of economic growth on a family's decisions about having children.

BACKGROUND

World population today stands at about 6.3 billion, compared with 2.5 billion in 1950 and only 1 billion in 1830. Demographers at the United Nations Population Fund estimate that by 2050, world population will reach 9 billion.

The population growth implied by these numbers has caused some observers to predict dire consequences, including famine and resource depletion, as more people demand more and more of everything. Many environmentalists recommend, accordingly, various policies aimed at cutting population growth throughout the world.

But population growth is not a uniform trend affecting all nations in the same way. Between 1950 and 1990, world population doubled, but only about 13 percent of the growth occurred in developed countries. Population growth in the next half-century will be concentrated, demographers say, in developing countries. Countries in Africa and south Asia will see the largest increases. Meanwhile, birth rates generally are low, and declining, in wealthier, developed nations. According to the Population Reference Bureau, Japan may lose 20 percent of its population in the next half-century, and Germany's population may decline by 9 percent. Moreover, the population in wealthy, developed nations is increasingly elderly. The combination of declining birth rates and an aging population strains the capacity of these nations to maintain their old-age retirement and health-care programs, since those programs are funded by taxes on the working-age population. In some wealthy, developed nations, accordingly, *under-*

population now looks like a serious problem.

ECOMYSTERY

Why do people in poor nations — who might seem to be the least able to afford the costs of raising children — have more children than people in rich nations?

ECONOMIC REASONING

In 1798, Thomas Robert Malthus wrote *An Essay on the Principle of Population as It Affects the Future Improvement of Society*. The book was a shocker. It contended that world population was increasing geometrically, while the food supply was increasing only arithmetically. Output of food could not keep up with population, therefore, and the world faced disaster in the form of mass starvation.

Modern Malthusians continue to predict disaster unless people worldwide act to limit population growth. Unless we limit growth, Paul Ehrlich wrote in 1968, "We will breed ourselves into oblivion."

The Malthusian predictions are based on something like the power of compounding. Population compounds like interest. Just as bank depositors receive interest on interest they have earned previously in a savings account, population growth gets added on to growth that has occurred previously. For example: If the population in a given town is 60,000 in 2004 and the annual growth rate is 5 percent, the population will grow to 63,000 people (1,000 x 1.05 = 63,000) by 2005. And if growth continues to increase at an annual rate of 5 percent, the population of that town will reach 66,150 people (63,000 x 1.05 = 66,150) by 2006.

As increases compound at this rate, the population goes up more quickly than you might think. How quickly? By dividing the annual rate of population growth into 70 (70/5, in the example above), you can calculate how long it would take the population to double. The answer here is 14 years (70/5 = 14), which predicts a population of 120,000 for the town in question by 2018. The same calculation performed for a larger initial population, or a higher growth rate, would of course predict correspondingly larger increases. Growth of this sort, Malthusians argue, will outstrip the supply of resources needed to feed, house and clothe the world's population.

Malthus wrote his analysis before the industrial revolution took hold in the nineteenth century. He was therefore unable to foresee how technology would affect food production (food production has generally increased, while food prices have decreased). His analysis assumes, moreover, that population will continue to grow at a geometric rate indefinitely. And it assumes that population growth brings only costs — no benefits — to the societies affected by it. That assumption has subsequently been challenged for various reasons. One reason has to do with the costs and benefits of bearing and raising children (EcoDetection principle 2). Those costs and benefits vary, depending on how poor or wealthy the family in question is.

For poor people living in a developing nation, the opportunity cost of having children may be low — if, for example, a parent (traditionally the mother) has no high-paying job she must give up in order to spend time raising her family. At the same time, the benefits that children bring to a poor family may be very valuable, since the children may work for or on behalf of the family, providing much-needed income. In wealthier, developed nations, on the other hand, parents who care for their children at home may pay a high opportunity cost in the form of wages not earned. Or they may pay high costs for childcare provided by others. Their children, moreover, are unlikely to work for or on behalf of the family, especially now that few children in developed nations grow up on family farms. And parents in developed nations are less likely than those in developing nations to be dependent on their children for care in old age.

As developing nations become more prosperous and poor people become increasingly able to earn good incomes, they will tend to have fewer children (EcoDetection principle 4). This trend has been observed in many different countries and cultural groups.

Economic Concepts

- Benefits
- Incentives
- Opportunity cost

Objectives

Students will:

1. Compare developing countries to developed countries by reference to birth rates, life-expectancy averages and infant-mortality rates.

2. Evaluate arguments about the effects of population growth, identifying possible costs and benefits.

3. Analyze the relationship between economic growth and birth rates by reference to the concept of *incentives*.

Content Standards

- Productive resources are limited. Therefore, people cannot have everything they want; as a result, they must choose some things and give up others. (NCEE Content Standard 1.)

- People respond predictably to positive and negative incentives. (NCEE Content Standard 4.)

- Income for most people is determined by the market value of the productive resources they sell. What workers earn depends, primarily, on the market value of what they produce and how productive they are. (NCEE standard 13.)

- Investment in factories, machinery, new technology, and the health, education, and training of people can raise future standards of living. (NCEE standard 15.)

Time

75 minutes

Materials

- A transparency of Visual 8.1
- A copy of Activities 8. 1 and 8.2 for each student

Procedure

A. Tell the class that this lesson focuses on what seems to be an odd fact: People living in poor, undeveloped nations tend to have more children than people living in wealthier, developed nations. **Display Visual 8.1** and invite the students to speculate about explanations for the mystery it presents. Explain that, in pursuing this mystery, the class will consider the costs and benefits of having children. The analysis will focus first on costs. To get started, ask the students what they think the costs of raising children have been for their parents — not the dollar amounts, but the cost categories.

Entertain all kinds of answers; make a list of representative responses on the chalkboard.

LESSON 8

B. The students probably will not have identified the *opportunity costs* of raising children.

If they have touched on opportunity costs, pick up on their response as a point of transition. If they have not, introduce the concept as it applies in this context.

Explain that the costs of raising children go far beyond paying for diapers, toys, daycare, clothing, dental work, books and tuition for school, and so on. These expenses are important, but another sort of cost is important too. Parents have only so much time and money. When they spend time and money on one activity or goal, they give up the chance to spend it on something else. What they give up — the next-best choice they would otherwise have made — is their *opportunity cost*. Depending on the circumstances and values of the parents in question, that opportunity cost might include income not earned from paid employment, home-cooked meals not prepared, recreation not enjoyed with adult friends, home renovations not undertaken, advanced education not pursued, and so on.

C. Then shift to a discussion of benefits. Ask the students how their parents benefit from raising them.

Again, entertain several answers, but emphasize non-monetary benefits such as enjoying children's company, being proud of the children's achievements, feeling invigorated by children's activity, and so on.

D. Summarize the discussion of costs and benefits: For many people who decide to raise children in our society, the costs are high. For devoted parents, of course, the benefits outweigh these costs. But the benefits for devoted parents are apt to be intangible (matters of affection, esteem or spiritual satisfaction, perhaps), whereas the costs may be more tangible (money spent on clothing and recreation, for example, as well as income not earned by parents who forgo working outside the home while they provide care for their own children).

E. Tell the students that the costs and benefits of having children may be different in different societies. **Distribute a copy of Activity 8.1** to each student. Discuss the information with the class to get them oriented to it. Explain terms as necessary:

- **Population density per square kilometer** is determined by dividing the country's area (in square kilometers) by the country's population.

The greater the population density per square kilometer, the more crowded the country.

- **Per capita GDP** is the value of all goods and services produced in a year, divided by the population. The higher the per capita GDP, the richer the nation. People in nations with high per capita GDPs have a higher standard of living than those in nations with low per capita GDPs.

- **Births per 1,000** is the number of babies born each year compared to the population. Population growth depends on this birth rate as compared to the death rate. (Only the birth rate is used in this lesson, however, to simplify the analysis.)

- **Female life expectancy** is a health indicator. The longer the life expectancy, the healthier the people of the country. A long life expectancy also usually means a lower death rate. This lesson uses female life expectancy to simplify the analysis. Female life expectancy is usually one or two years longer than male life expectancy.

- **Infant mortality per 1,000 live births** is another health measure. It is the number of deaths to infants under one year of age, in a given year, per 1,000 live births in the same year. Nations with low infant mortality rates have higher health standards and a higher standard of living than nations with high infant mortality rates.

F. After the preliminary discussion, divide the class into small groups; assign the groups to study the information further and to answer the questions in Part 1.

G. Discuss the answers to the questions in Part 1. Answers follow:

1. *U.S.A., Switzerland, Canada, Belgium and Japan*
2. *177 people per square kilometer*
3. *11 per 1,000 people*
4. *4.6 per 1,000 live births*
5. *82.4 years*
6. *Afghanistan, Bangladesh, Ethiopia, Somalia and Congo (Democratic Republic of)*
7. *47.1 people per square kilometer*
8. *40.4 per 1,000 people*
9. *106 per 1,000 live births*
10. *49.8 years*

H. On the chalkboard, summarize a main point: The numbers show higher birth rates for the poorer nations. Now the task is to figure out why that might be so. To pursue this task, the students will look first at a letter written by an immigrant farmer in Wisconsin in 1854. **Distribute a copy of Activity 8.2** to each student. Ask the students to read the letter and respond to the Questions for Discussion. Answers follow:

1. *The Hoefer children worked at many jobs for or on behalf of the family. Michel, Phillip and Lena worked in Pittsburgh. Michel and Phillip worked with Mr. Hoefer on another farmer's harvest. Lena took a job as a domestic servant for an English family; Phillip also worked for that family, and Minnie worked for a relative of the family. Unspecified family members worked to build a barn and a house. Michel and Phillip worked harvesting the family's fields. And unspecified family members hunted together to put meat on the family's table.*

2. *Mr. Hoefer needed Michel to work directly on the family farm. He could not afford to give up Michel's labor at the rate offered. The opportunity cost of allowing Michel to work outside the family would have been too high.*

3. *We do not know exactly how old the Hoefer children were, nor do we know whether schools were available to them at the time in rural Wisconsin. These factors may help to explain Mr. Hoefer's inattention to schooling in his letter. But the value of the work performed by his children might well have outweighed the value of schooling, in Mr. Hoefer's eyes, even if schools had been available to his school-age children. For the Hoefer family, in other words, the opportunity cost of school attendance might have made schooling seem prohibitively expensive.*

4. *In stating that he had "not enough children" in this country, Mr. Hoefer acknowledges that, in his family, children provided valuable benefits. They worked for and on behalf of the Hoefer family. More Hoefer children would have meant more benefits.*

I. Summarize a main point from Activity 8.1: Mr. Hoefer knew that his family benefited by having many children. The children could do valuable work for and on behalf of their family. Also, the opportunity cost of that family-oriented work was apparently very low, since Mr. Hoefer does not identify better opportunities the children might have focused on instead.

J. Might the Hoefer explanation apply more broadly — to people raising large families in developing nations today? We have no letters written by poor farmers in Bangladesh or Somalia to refer to, but we do have information about rich and poor nations, and we can look at that information in order to make inferences about how well the Hoefer explanation might apply in various places. Ask the students to return to their groups; assign the groups to answer the questions in Activity 8.1, Part 2. When they have finished, call on a representative from each group to report to the class; then have the class discuss each question. Possible answers follow:

1. *Poor nations have higher birth rates. The reasons may be similar to Mr. Hoefer's reasons: The benefits of having many children to work for and on behalf of the family are probably great, and — in economic environments where opportunities are meager — the opportunity costs are probably low.*

2. *Birth rates decline as nations grow wealthier. Why? In part because strong economic growth provides opportunities for individuals to obtain better-paying jobs. In such an economic context, the opportunity cost of taking time to bear and raise children goes up. As costs go up, women on average have fewer children.*

3. *The quality of life is much better in rich nations. In rich countries, infant mortality rates are lower, and people have longer life expectancies.*

4. *Economic growth creates incentives for people to have smaller rather than larger families. Birth rates tend to go down, therefore, as nations develop and become more prosperous. The quality of life — as measured by infant mortality rates and life expectancy — improves as economic growth increases prosperity.*

LESSON 8

CLOSURE

Refocus attention on the mystery underlying this lesson: Why do people in poor nations tend to have more children than people in wealthier nations? Call on the students to explain how each of the following concepts relates to this question:

- Opportunity cost

  All decisions involve opportunity cost. The decision to bear and raise children is no exception. Where the opportunity costs of bearing and raising children are seen as high, birth rates tend to be low.

- Benefits

  In making decisions, people weigh costs against benefits. Here, too, the decision to bear and raise children is no exception. Where people believe that they benefit by having many children, birth rates tend to be high.

- Incentives

  In weighing the costs and benefits of having more or fewer children, people are influenced by incentives. Abundant economic opportunities for men and women in a given society create an incentive for adults in that society to seek paid employment outside the home. Such opportunities increase the opportunity cost of bearing and raising children, since parents who choose to spend time on parenting could spend that time in paid employment instead. Economic growth and prosperity, therefore, are associated with low birth rates.

ASSESSMENT

Multiple-Choice Questions

1. Which of the following statements is true?

   a. People in rich nations have fewer children than people in poor nations.

   b. Nations with many people per square kilometer are usually poor.

   c. Because it has fewer people per square kilometer, China is richer than Hong Kong.

   d. People live longer in poor countries because the environment is much cleaner than the environment in industrialized rich countries.

2. Which of the following occurs when nations become richer?

   a. The environment becomes dirtier.

   b. The birth rate falls.

   c. Life expectancy decreases.

   d. The possibility of starvation increases.

Essay Questions

1. Why are birth rates higher in poor countries than in rich countries?

Large families often provide benefits for people living in developing nations, since family members may be employed in working directly for or on behalf of the family, contributing to the family's income. Also, for people living in places where economic opportunities are few, the opportunity cost of employing children in family-oriented work, or of adults in parenting, may be low. When economic opportunities improve, however, the incentives change. Adults in wealthy, developed nations may pay a heavy opportunity cost if they choose to take time off from work to bear and raise children, and children growing up in wealthy, developed nations do not usually work for or on behalf of their families in the way that many children do in developing nations.

2. Government officials in Country A are concerned about high birth rates and overpopulation. Most people in Country A are poor, and women there traditionally do not work except in their homes or farm fields. The Minister of Education for Country A proposes a long-range plan to provide a system of public education and vocational training that will be made available, for the first time in the country's history, to all children, male and female. If such a plan could be implemented, how might it affect Country A's birth rate? Explain your answer by reference to the concept of *opportunity cost*.

Women who qualify for paid employment forfeit benefits (including income, status and the satisfaction some find in workplace participation) when they do not go to work. As women in Country A begin to acquire education and vocational training, they will begin to qualify for paid employment. As they qualify for paid employment, they will be less inclined to raise large families. The opportunity cost of time spent raising large families — lost income and the loss of status and satisfaction that some women otherwise would have gained through work — will seem too high.

VISUAL 8.1

WHY ARE THERE MORE CHILDREN WHERE WE MIGHT EXPECT TO FIND FEWER?

Why do people in poor countries — who might seem to be the least able to afford the costs of raising children — have more children than people in wealthier countries?

LESSON 8

ACTIVITY 8.1

A TALE OF 20 NATIONS

Name_____

Directions: Examine the statistics shown in the table below. Respond to the questions in Parts 1 and 2 on the next page.

Nation	Population density per square kilometer	Per capita GDP (in $)	Births per 1,000	Life expectancy female	Infant mortality per 1,000 live births
Afghanistan	44	700	41	46	143
Bangladesh	96	1,700	30	61	67
Belgium	337	29,000	10	82	4
Canada	3	29,400	11	83	5
China	129	4,400	13	74	25
Congo, Dem. Republic	24	610	45	51	97
Ethiopia	59	750	40	42	103
France	110	25,700	13	83	4
Germany	231	26,600	9	82	4
Haiti	271	1,701	34	53	76
Hong Kong	671	26,000	11	83	6
Japan	337	28,000	10	84	3
Mexico	53	9,000	22	76	24
Singapore	6,650	24,000	13	84	4
Somalia	12.6	550	46	49	120
Switzerland	177	31,700	10	83	4
Taiwan	628	18,000	13	80	7
Uganda	109	1260	47	47	88
U.K.	245	25,300	11	81	5
U.S. A.	30	37,600	14	80	7

*Source: CIA World FactBook, 2003. Numbers rounded to the nearest whole number.

ACTIVITY 8.1, CONTINUED

Questions for Discussion

In your small group, choose a representative to take notes and report the results of your discussion to the class. Then discuss and record your responses to the following questions.

PART 1: ANALYZING DATA

1. Which five nations have the highest per capita GDP?

   We will consider these nations rich.

2. What is the average population density per square kilometer of these five rich nations?

   Hint: Add up the population density figures for the five nations and divide by five.

3. What is the average birth rate per 1,000 people for these five rich nations?

   Hint: Add up the birth rate figures for the five nations and divide by five.

4. What is the average infant mortality rate per 1,000 live births for these five rich nations?

   Hint: Add up the infant mortality rate figures for the five nations and divide by five.

5. What is the average female life expectancy for these five rich nations?

   You shouldn't need a hint by now.

6. Which five nations have the lowest per capita GDP?

   We will consider these nations poor.

7. What is the average population density per square kilometer for these five poor nations?

8. What is the average birth rate per 1,000 people for these five poor nations?

9. What is the average infant mortality rate per 1,000 live births for these five poor nations?

10. What is the average female life expectancy for these five poor nations?

PART 2: DRAWING CONCLUSIONS

1. Do rich nations or poor nations have a higher average birth rate? Why?

2. What will probably happen to population growth as nations become richer?

3. How does the quality of life in poor nations compare to the quality of life in rich nations?

   Use statistics from the table to support your answer.

4. How is economic growth related to birth rates and quality of life?

LESSON 8

ACTIVITY 8.2

IN THIS COUNTRY I HAVE NOT ENOUGH CHILDREN

Name_____

Nicolaus Hoefer, a nineteenth-century immigrant to Sauk County, Wisconsin, wrote the following letter in 1854. (The letter, written originally in Geman, is personal correspondence in the possession of Mr. Hoefer's great-great grand-children.) Addressed to his relatives and friends in Nasstaten, Germany, the letter tells how the Hoefer family managed to get settled in a new homeland. Read the letter, paying special attention to Mr. Hoefer's account of how family members worked together to enable the family to prosper. Then respond to the Questions for Discussion.

Retzburg, Sauk County, Wisc.
November 1854

Dear Parents, Brothers and Sisters, Father-in-law, Brother-in-law, Friends and Acquaintances:

With great pleasure I take the pen to report that I, my wife and children are all hale and hearty and hope you will all be well as you receive this....I must also write how we are faring and how we like it in America.

Our voyage across the ocean was completed....happily and in good health. It took 33 days from London to New York, from there we went to Pittsburgh, where we stayed during the winter. Fourteen days we had no work, then Michel and Phillip got work in the city. Michel got twenty dollars and Phillip fifteen dollars a month, Lena one dollar and twenty-five cents and Elizabeth one dollar a week. I did not work but looked around Pittsburgh for land, but in vain....Then I went on a trip to Wisconsin.

The trip from Pittsburgh to Wisconsin took five weeks by water. I bought 120 acres of land for one and one-fourth dollars an acre....

Because I was by myself and could do no work on my land, I came to a farmer who had three farms, two in the woods and one in the prairie. On each farm was a house and barn. I rented one in the woods with house and barn and four acres of garden ground....When my wife and children came, I had already planted potatoes, Indian corn, beans, lettuce and other seeds. I bought two cows with calves, six hogs and nine chickens....

Thanks and glory to God, food and clothing and also money I do not lack, for we planted many vegetables in our garden, more than we needed. Everything grows easily....

Only mentioning a few things, how many could I name!....Our bread I earned during the harvest when I worked for a farmer on the prairie. I and my two sons earned every day....six bushels [of wheat]....We earned during the harvest more than 109 bushels....So we have money....

My daughter, Lena, when here a short time, there came a young man — he was English, he was married and had a wife and child, and [he] took [Lena] along as a servant girl in his home, which is only three miles from us. She gets a dollar and a half a week. Shortly after Harvest, the same man came and got Phillip, who gets ten dollars a month during the winter. Elizabeth is [working for] these folks' parents and gets a dollar a week. At the same time they are all three learning English. Next summer

ACTIVITY 8.2, CONTINUED

when they speak English they will earn more. Minnie shall work by [the English woman's] sister. Michel can get fourteen dollars [a month], but I cannot spare him.

Dear folks, behold in this country I have not enough children. When in Germany, a father and mother who have seven children as I here — there one does not know where to put them to support themselves, but in America it is far different....The boys, after working one year, can buy eighty acres...and have money left....I and my oldest son work on our farm. We have built a house. Now we are building a barn....I have rented fourteen acres of land in addition to [the land I own]....There we sowed twelve bushels of wheat....

The Americans do things easily and quickly. The wheat is cut with a cradle. A person swings it and goes half a step forward, and....another one ties the wheat after him....They also cut with machines and then it takes eight men to tie the grain. Threshing the grain is also done quickly. My two sons and I [were] helped by a machine, when 300 bushels of wheat were threshed in a day; 400 bushels of oats can be threshed in a day, for which are needed two horses and eight to ten men. Michel and I work on our farm.

When we are tired, we take our guns and go hunting, for there are many deers, rabbits, pheasants and prairie chickens....

Dear parents, brothers and sisters, father-in-law, friends and acquaintances: if one or other of you would like to come, come. You are welcome!

Nicolaus Hoefer

Questions for Discussion

1. In what ways did the Hoefer sons and daughters work for or on behalf of the family?

2. Mr. Hoefer tells of an opportunity Michel had to earn $14 a month. That seems to have been a good wage, compared to what the others earned. But Mr. Hoefer would not allow Michel to take this job: "I cannot spare him," he explains. What does he mean by that? Why did he not want Michel to earn $14 a month?

3. Mr. Hoefer seems to appreciate the value of learning. He is literate himself, and he is pleased to note that his children have begun to learn English. But he does not speak of sending any of his children to school, nor does he express any regret about their absence from school. What might his reasons be for this apparent lack of concern about schooling?

4. Mr. Hoefer states that "in this country I have not enough children." Why does he make that statement? Explain.

LESSON 9

WHY DO OIL RESERVES KEEP INCREASING?

LESSON 9

WHY DO OIL RESERVES KEEP INCREASING?

LESSON DESCRIPTION

The students view a visual regarding oil reserves and consumption. They calculate how many years it will take us to run out of oil at a given rate of consumption. The teacher then explains that the numbers on the visual were from 1970 and that in the meanwhile we have not run out of oil. How can this be? The students learn the meaning of *provable reserves of petroleum* and use economic reasoning to explain why we have not run out of oil.

BACKGROUND

The physical quantity of petroleum in the world is fixed. It was created by changes that took place in the environment millions of years ago. From this fixed quantity we pump millions of barrels every day to be refined and sold worldwide so that people can drive cars, use electricity, fertilize their food and wear wrinkle-proof clothing.

Many environmentalists are concerned about the use of fossil fuels. Using fossil fuels pollutes the land and air; it may also make us dependent on a source of energy that will be unsustainable in the future.

The underlying question is whether we are in danger of running out of fossil fuels. In 1970 it seemed that perhaps we were. Environmental groups and government officials then expressed concern upon learning that provable oil reserves were 531 billion barrels and we were consuming 16.5 billion barrels annually. At that rate, we would run out of oil in about 30 years. Today, however, world reserves of crude oil are estimated at over 1 trillion barrels.

EcoMYSTERY

How could world reserves of oil (a nonrenewable resource) have increased over the past 35 years when greater amounts of oil are being burned every day?

ECONOMIC REASONING

The core misunderstandings here are two: first, that we know how much oil is available under the earth's crust; and second, that the *physical supply* and the *economic supply* of oil are the same thing.

Oil supplies are measured as *provable reserves at current prices and technology levels*. As prices rise or the costs of extraction go down, suppliers are given greater incentives to find more oil and list it as provable reserves (EcoDetection principle 4). Rising prices also encourage suppliers to extract oil that was previously known to exist but considered too difficult to obtain.

We have no idea what the physical amount of petroleum concealed by the earth's crust might be. But we do know something about the physical amount of petroleum that people now have an incentive to find. The amount that people are willing to find will change as incentives change.

ECONOMIC CONCEPTS

- Incentive
- Price
- Supply

OBJECTIVES

Students will:

1. Define the concept of *provable reserves of petroleum*.

2. Explain the relationship of incentives to the amount of petroleum available to the public.

3. Explain how a nonrenewable resource such as petroleum can increase in availability while huge amounts of it are being consumed.

CONTENT STANDARDS

- People respond predictably to positive and negative incentives. (NCEE Content Standard 4.)

- Markets exist when buyers and sellers interact. This interaction determines market prices and thereby allocates scarce goods and services. (NCEE Content Standard 7.)

- Prices send signals and provide incentives to buyers and sellers. When supply or demand changes, market prices adjust, affecting incentives. (NCEE Content Standard 8.)

TIME

45 minutes

MATERIALS

• A transparency of Visual 9.1, 9.2, 9.3, 9.4 and 9.5

PROCEDURE

A. Explain that the purpose of this lesson is to explore a mystery related to oil. People everywhere use more oil every year, yet we don't seem to be running out of oil. In fact, what is called the provable reserve supply of oil has increased over the past 35 years. How can this be?

B. **Display Visual 9.1** and pose the question to the class. Invite the students to calculate how many years it will take for the world to run out of crude oil. Tell the students they may use calculators if they wish. The students should estimate that it will take the world about 30 years to run out of oil at this rate of consumption.

C. **Display Visual 9.2.** Tell the students that the situation described in Visual 9.1 was based on oil reserves and consumption rates as of 1970. According to the calculations suggested at that time, we should have run out of oil by now. But we haven't run out. Today, provable reserves have grown to over a trillion barrels of oil — nearly double the reserves estimated in 1970 — and we are consuming more oil now than we did then.

D. Explain that in order to understand the change in oil reserves, we need to know what the *provable reserve supply* of oil is. **Display Visual 9.3.** Explain that provable reserves are determined by how much fossil fuel has been discovered and how much can be extracted with today's technology. Ask: What does knowing the amount of provable reserves tell us about how much of a natural resource still remains?

Not much. Provable reserves can change, for example, if technological improvements make new levels of extraction possible.

E. **Display Visual 9.4.** Discuss the pattern of large increases in oil reserves compared to modest increases in consumption.

F. Explain that the answer to the mystery lies in understanding how incentives affect the supply of provable reserves. **Display Visual 9.5** and discuss the incentives for producers and consumers. Ask:

• How do prices create incentives for producers of natural resources like petroleum?

Increased prices for a resource send signals about the potential for increased rewards. The potential for increased rewards encourages producers to find more of the resource and to develop new technology for extracting the resource.

• Why do producers develop new technology for extracting resources?

Producers want to earn profits. One way to increase profits is to reduce costs. Technology often enables producers to reduce costs.

• What incentives do consumers face when prices for petroleum-related products, such as gasoline, begin to increase?

When prices for petroleum-related products increase, consumers have an incentive to conserve. When gasoline prices go up steeply, consumers drive less, use mass transportation more, form car pools and begin to purchase more fuel-efficient cars.

G. **Display Visual 9.1** again and review the mystery. Ask the students to use the principles of EcoDetection to explain how the amount of oil (a nonrenewable resource) can increase when huge amounts of it are burned every day.

Oil companies' choices are influenced by incentives. As oil companies explore for oil, they know that estimates of provable reserves refer only to oil that can be recovered today. As prices and technology change, these reserve estimates increase or decrease. Reserve estimates do not reveal how much oil remains beneath the earth's crust. No one knows how much oil there is in that sense, but the amount is much greater than the reserve estimates indicate.

CLOSURE

Summarize the key points of the lesson. Estimates of provable reserves are not accurate estimates of the physical quantity of fossil fuel beneath the earth's crust. People's choices are influenced by incentives. Estimates of fossil fuel reserves change when the incentives to produce change. These incentives are affected by changing prices and technology.

Lesson 9

ASSESSMENT

Multiple-Choice Questions

1. Which of the following statements is false?

   a. Petroleum is a fossil fuel.

   b. Provable reserves of petroleum have increased from 1948 to 1995.

   c. People around the world are using more petroleum.

   d. The available amount of petroleum is decreasing.

2. Which of the following answers describes an incentive to produce oil?

   a. Consumers decide to use less oil.

   b. Businesses decide to use less oil.

   c. Governments decide to use less oil.

   d. Higher prices are paid for oil.

Essay Questions

1. Read the following statement. Tell whether you think it is accurate. Explain your answer.

"Oil is a nonrenewable resource. In 10 years we will not have any oil left to use for gas in our automobiles."

Petroleum is a nonrenewable resource as we presently produce it. It comes from fossil remains in the earth's crust. But we have several decades of provable reserves remaining. Provable reserves have increased since 1948, and they are likely to increase more. Also, we have not found all the reserves that exist in the earth's crust.

2. Read the following statement. Write a reply, using the concepts of *provable reserves* and *incentives* to help the writer understand this problem better.

"I can't believe statistics these days. Provable reserves of petroleum are greater now than 1948. But petroleum is limited. We have been using it heavily since 1948. How can it keep increasing when we use so much of it?"

The writer doesn't understand what "provable reserves" means. "Provable reserves" refers to the amount of petroleum available at today's prices and by means of today's technology. Provable reserves can increase if incentives such as higher prices or lower costs encourage producers to find and extract more petroleum. The numbers are not influenced by how much petroleum we have already used.

VISUAL 9.1

HOW LONG WILL THE WORLD'S OIL LAST?

Imagine this situation:

- Provable oil reserves stand at 531 billion barrels.

- The world is consuming 16.5 billion barrels each year.

How many years will it take for us out run out of oil?

Visual 9.2

How Long Will the World's Oil Last? Longer Than You Think!

- In 1970, provable oil reserves were 531 billion barrels.

- At 1970 rates of consumption, many people thought that we would run out of oil by the year 2000.

- Today we consume over 26 billion barrels of oil per year.

- Oil reserves today are over 1 trillion barrels.

- Almost certainly, we will never pump the last barrel of oil out of the earth.

- How can this be?

VISUAL 9.3

DEFINITION OF PROVABLE RESERVES

Provable reserves of fossil fuels such as coal, gas and oil, include only those amounts that have already been discovered and amounts can be extracted by means of present technology at current prices.

VISUAL 9.4

WORLD OIL RESERVES AND CONSUMPTION

Reserves

Year	Barrels (in billions)
1980	645
1990	1,002
2002	1,032

Average Consumption

Year	Thousand barrels per day
1980	63,067
1990	66,083
2002	77,659

Source: Energy Information Administration

VISUAL 9.5

SOLVING THE MYSTERY:
PEOPLE'S CHOICES ARE INFLUENCED BY INCENTIVES

Producers:

- How do prices create incentives for producers of natural resources like petroleum?

- Why do producers develop new technology for extracting resources?

Consumers:

- What incentives do consumers face when prices for petroleum-related products, such as gasoline, begin to increase?

LESSON 10

WHY DRIVE WHEN YOU CAN RIDE?

LESSON 10

WHY DRIVE WHEN YOU CAN RIDE?

LESSON DESCRIPTION

The students examine data showing that many Americans prefer to drive their own automobiles rather than use mass public transit. They analyze this preference by reference to the costs and benefits of driving. In light of the external costs generated by automobile travel, the students evaluate market-oriented proposals for decreasing those costs.

BACKGROUND

Americans get around. They spend more than $1 trillion annually on transportation products and services. Transportation expenditures accounted for 10.8 percent of Gross Domestic Product (GDP) in 2000, about the same percentage that Americans spent on food.

For most Americans, travel by automobile, including sport utility vehicles, is the preferred mode. Ninety percent of Americans have access to a motor vehicle, according to the U.S. Census Bureau, and half the nation's households have two or more vehicles. Motor vehicle registrations in the United States have increased from about 74 million in 1960 to about 217 million in 2001. In getting to work, about 88 percent of Americans in 2000 traveled by car — as compared with 64 percent in 1960. Only 4.7 percent of workers (in 2000) traveled to work via public transit.

As popular as motor-vehicle travel is, its large presence in American life causes problems. Ninety percent of transportation fatalities in the United States result from automobile accidents. On congested streets and highways, travelers often find themselves caught in gridlock. Emissions from automobile engines contribute to air pollution. And easy access to cars and freeways has helped to lure many Americans away from homes in urban areas into what critics call sprawling suburbs, where cornfields and woodlots have given way to strip malls and tract housing.

In response to problems of this sort, urban planners and environmentalists have proposed a host of policies including more stringent fuel-efficiency standards, controls on development in neighborhoods with single-family homes, urban-growth boundaries intended to restrict construction near the outskirts of certain cities, and extensive subsidies for public transit. But public transit, in particular, has been a tough sell. It accounted for 51 percent of all urban travel in 1945; today it accounts only for 3 percent of urban travel. Despite its significant presence in certain metropolitan areas, it plays no part in the lives of most Americans.

ECOMYSTERY

Why do so many Americans stick almost exclusively to travel by automobile? In light of widespread concern about air quality, resource depletion, and day-to-day problems of traffic congestion, why haven't they shown more support for public transit and come to use it more extensively?

ECONOMIC REASONING

In deciding to drive rather than use mass transit, Americans are influenced by incentives (EcoDetection principle 4). One incentive is low costs. The federal and state governments help to keep the cost of driving low (EcoDetection principle 5). They do this by providing freeways paid for by all the taxpayers. Taxpayers who drive little or not at all thus help to pay for streets and highways used extensively by others who drive all the time. Because travel by automobile is subsidized in this way, Americans have an incentive to drive. For individual drivers, moreover, the benefits of driving — in convenience and flexibility, for example — may be considerable.

What looks like a set of rational choices to individuals, however, may nonetheless impose costs on others, including the costs of dealing with engine emissions and traffic congestion (EcoDetection principle 3). Market-oriented solutions to these problems of external costs would require drivers to pay more fully for the actual costs generated by their driving (EcoDetection principle 2).

ECONOMIC CONCEPTS

- Benefit
- Cost
- Externality

OBJECTIVES

Students will:

1. Use a cost/benefit analysis to explain why Americans generally remain attached to travel by automobiles rather than public transit.

2. Evaluate approaches to reducing the external costs of travel by automobile.

CONTENT STANDARDS

- Productive resources are limited. Therefore, people cannot have everything they want; as a result, they must choose some things and give up others. (NCEE Content Standard 1.)

- People respond predictably to positive and negative incentives. (NCEE Content Standard 4.)

- Prices send signals and provide incentives to buyers and sellers. When supply or demand changes, market prices adjust, affecting incentives. (NCEE Content Standard 8.)

TIME

75 minutes

MATERIALS

- A transparency of Visuals 10.1, 10.2, 10.3 and 10.4
- A copy of Activities 10.1 and 10.2 for each student

PROCEDURE

A. Explain that the purpose of this lesson is to explore what some people have called America's love affair with cars. It is something that can be illustrated in various ways — by reference to the eagerness of most young people to obtain drivers' licenses as soon as they can, for example, or by reference to popular imagery in movies and advertisements in which sleek, powerful cars are associated with success and glamour, or simply by reference to the crowded roads and parking lots many people encounter every day.

B. The large presence of cars in American life can be quantified by various statistics. One such statistic has to do with how Americans get to work. Ask the students to take their best guess at the percentage Americans who drive to work every day, as compared to the percentage riding public tran-

sit. Record a sample of their estimates on the chalkboard. Then project a transparency of **Visual 10.1.** Compare the information it presents with the students' estimates. Discuss the trends revealed in the national data, noting the increase in use of personal vehicles and the decrease in use of public transit since 1960.

C. Next, ask the "so what" question: Americans are strongly attached to their cars, but why should that be a matter of concern? What reason is there for worrying about the preference shown by most Americans for travel by automobile?

Students may mention gas guzzlers and fuel consumption, air pollution, traffic congestion, land-use issues.

D. Acknowledge the importance of these concerns. Emphasize the point that, because that these concerns are important, it seems especially puzzling that Americans persist in relying heavily on their cars rather than increasing their demand for and use of various forms of public mass transit. **Display Visual 10.2.** What might explain this mystery?

Responses will vary. List representative responses on the chalkboard.

E. Unless the students have mentioned it themselves, add *cost* to the list of possible explanations. In order to introduce the role of cost as a factor, project a transparency of **Visual 10.3.** Ask the students what the three situations represented there have in common.

In each case, a service is provided at no charge. High demand for the three events reflects the low cost of participation. (Participation still isn't free, since it costs people at least some time and effort.) People generally want more of things when costs are low.

F. What does all this have to do with crowded freeways and parking lots? Explain the important point of similarity between driving cars and attending low-cost entertainment events. Streets and highways cost a lot of money to build and maintain and patrol. The costs are borne by government — local, state and federal. Highway users cover some of these costs through the taxes they pay. The share of costs they cover, according to *Highway Statistics* (2001), is about 65 percent. In other words, government subsidies reduce the cost of driving by 35 percent. If drivers had to

LESSON 10

cover 100 percent of the costs of driving, or something closer to 100 percent, they would presumably drive less.

G. But hold on. Public transit is subsidized too. Project **Visual 10. 4.** Discuss the information it presents. Ask: If subsidies increase demand for automobile travel by reducing costs for drivers, why haven't subsidies for public transit increased the demand for travel by light rail and commuter trains?

The students may mention poor access to public transit in some areas, inconvenience of having to travel according to a transit schedule, and so on.

H. Picking up on the students' responses, refocus the discussion on *benefits* as a second factor to consider in trying to explain the strong attachment many Americans feel to their cars. Distribute copies of **Activity 10.1.** Ask the students to read the account of Ms. Rosado's commuting; then ask them to respond to the question the Activity poses. Discuss their responses.

In identifying benefits, the students may include convenience, time saved, flexibility, privacy.

I. Emphasize the point that many individuals like Ms. Rosado choose to drive because the benefits they experience individually — in convenience and flexibility — outweigh the costs. Then explain that this analysis of individual costs and benefits doesn't tell the whole story. In choosing to drive to work — and, generally, in relying on cars for transportation — Ms. Rosado and millions of other individuals also generate costs that are imposed on others. Those costs include the costs of dealing with emissions from automobile engines, the costs of managing traffic and dealing with accidents, and the costs of highway construction and maintenance. Costs of this sort are called *external costs* or *externalities* because they are not borne directly by the people who generate them. External costs associated with individual decisions may be high, even when those decisions look perfectly rational from an individual's point of view.

J. Turn to the final major question posed in this lesson: What steps might be taken to decrease the external costs associated with automobile travel in the United States? Efforts to date have focused on certain regulations (for emissions control and fuel

efficiency, for example) and on promoting public transit. Results have been mixed:

- Fuel efficiency for passenger cars has improved steadily between 1955 and 2000 (source: *National Transportation Statistics 2000* [2001]), and emission levels for three important pollutants monitored by the Environmental Protection Agency (carbon monoxide, nitrogen oxides and volatile organic compounds) have decreased steadily (source: EPA, *Average Annual Emissions* [2003]).

- But fuel efficiency is generally much poorer for the sport utility vehicles and light trucks favored by an increasing number of drivers, and Americans have decreased their use of public transit even as efforts to promote it have increased.

K. People interested in reducing the external costs of automobile travel have therefore sought to identify other alternatives. Two such alternatives are described briefly on Activity 10.2. Distribute copies of **Activity 10.2** and ask the students to read the two proposals it presents. Then divide the class into small groups; assign the groups to respond to the question: Which external costs of automobile travel would each proposal address? Which external costs would each proposal fail to address?

Congestion-based pricing: might reduce congestion; might decrease fuel consumption and emissions caused by cars caught in traffic gridlock; would not otherwise address fuel consumption or air-quality issues. HOT lanes: might reduce congestion, along with fuel consumption and emissions caused by cars caught in traffic gridlock; would not otherwise address fuel consumption or air-quality issues.

CLOSURE

Display Visual 10.2 again and call on students to solve the mystery it poses, using the concepts of *costs, benefits,* and *externalities* in their answers. The students' answers should reflect understanding of points summarized below.

- *Costs: Government subsidies of automobile travel reduce costs for individual drivers, creating an incentive to drive. The federal government and local governments also subsidize public transit, but despite these subsidies the use of public transit has dwindled since World War II.*

- **Benefits:** *Individuals associate many benefits with automobile travel, including convenience, mobility, flexibility and privacy.*

- **Externalities:** *While the decision to drive looks perfectly rational to many individuals, automobile travel generates some costs that must be paid for externally — that is, by people at large. These externalities include the costs of dealing with emissions from automobile engines and the costs of traffic congestion. Emissions problems have been addressed in part through government regulation. Market-oriented solutions have been proposed for problems of congestion, but little has been done to implement such proposals to date.*

ASSESSMENT

Multiple-Choice Questions

1. Airlines are often accused of creating noise pollution and congestion during peak travel times — mornings and evenings. What would an EcoDetective advise us to do to reduce noise and congestion caused by air travel?

   a. Pass a law requiring reduced noise and congestion.

   b. Impose a special tax on the purchase of airline tickets.

   c. Use a system of congestion-based pricing to set landing fees for airlines.

   d. Include instruction about the effects of noise pollution in all K-12 school programs.

2. Tollways, toll charges at exit ramps, and parking fees are devices requiring individual drivers to help pay for the costs they impose on

   a. themselves.

   b. immigrants.

   c. other drivers.

   d. their children.

Essay Questions

1. What are some of the costs individuals pay when they drive on busy freeways? What are the costs for which individual drivers do not pay? Discuss these questions in a brief essay.

Individuals usually pay for the purchase and maintenance of their cars, plus expenses related to fuel, car repairs and insurance. They also pay various taxes, generating revenue that goes to help pay for highway construction and maintenance. Costs imposed on others, for which they do not pay full freight, include costs related to air pollution, noise pollution and traffic congestion.

2. Leon's mother usually drives on the freeway to work. Leon tells her that she should carpool with one of her friends. She tells Leon about getting Leon's brother to daycare and trips she must make to the bank, grocery store and video store. She gets angry whenever Leon mentions carpooling. Propose an alternative policy that might encourage Leon's mother to reduce her driving voluntarily. Explain your proposed policy by reference to costs and benefits.

Leon's mother benefits from using the freeway. These benefits cost her relatively little. The combination of low costs and important benefits helps to explain why Leon's mother prefers to drive. She might be encouraged to drive less if she had to pay more, and pay more directly, for the driving she does — by paying a toll for peak-period uses of freeways, for example.

VISUAL 10.1

HOW AMERICANS GET TO WORK: NATIONAL DATA, 1960-2000

	Total Trips	Number and percent by personal vehicles (primarily cars)	Number and percent by public transit
1960	64,655,805	41,368,062 (64%)	7,806,932 (12.1%)
1970	76,852,389	59,722,550 (77.7%)	6,810,458 (8.9%)
1980	96,617,296	81,258,496 (84.1%)	6,175,061 (6.4%)
1990	115,070,274	99,592,932 (86.5%)	6,069,589 (5.3%)
2000	128,279,228	112,736,101 (87.9%)	6,067,703 (4.7%)

Source: Urban Transport Fact Book (various years)

VISUAL 10.2

THE MYSTERY OF THE AUTOMOBILE DRIVERS WHO JUST WON'T QUIT

Why do so many Americans stick almost exclusively to travel by automobile? In light of widespread concern about air quality, resource depletion and day-to-day problems of traffic congestion, why haven't they shown more support for public transit and come to use it much more extensively?

VISUAL **10.3**

IT SURE GETS CROWDED SOMETIMES

- Townsend, Wisconsin, is famous for its spectacular Fourth of July fireworks display, sponsored and funded by local merchants. Local residents and tourists crowd into the town park to watch the display. Many of them position their blankets or lawn chairs hours in advance of the 9:30 p.m. starting time in order to stake out their viewing turf. Cars are parked everywhere, often illegally. As 9:30 approaches, a crowd of viewers far larger than the little town's population waits for the first sky rocket to signal the start of the show.

- To generate publicity for a new blockbuster movie, Disney sets up giant movie screens in New York's Central Park and invites everyone to watch the new film — no charge for admission. The areas around the screens are packed tight with movie fans.

- The Roadkill Warrior Maniacs, a rock band eager to earn its 15 minutes of fame, gives a concert in a farmer's pasture. There is no charge for admission. The band's fans arrive in droves.

Question for Discussion

What do these situations have in common?

VISUAL 10.4

PUBLIC TRANSIT FUNDING AND USAGE TRENDS

- In 1964, the first U.S. Urban Mass Transportation Act was passed. At that time, about nine percent of urban person-miles of travel were made via public transit. Today, about three percent of urban person-miles of travel are made via public transit.

- Since the federal government became involved in subsidizing local public transit in 1964, more than $100 billion in federal dollars have gone into those systems. Over this same period, local governments have put more than $265 billion into subsidizing public transit systems.

- For 2001, government at all levels spent about $40 billion on public transit.

- Given these subsidies, the share of public transit operating costs covered by passenger fares averages out to about 30 percent. In other words, users of public transit pay about 30 percent of the cost of their rides; non-users pay the other 70 percent.

- Despite this subsidy from federal and local funding, annual per capita public transit trips have declined from 43 in 1965 to 33 in 2000.

Sources: Public Transportation Fact Book (2003); *Statistical Abstract* (2000)

ACTIVITY **10.1**

DRIVING TO WORK: DAYS IN THE LIFE OF MARIA ROSADO

Name_____

Read the account of Ms. Rosado's commuting. Then respond to the Question for Discussion.

Maria Rosado lives on the south side of Milwaukee, Wisconsin, with her two children. She works for the Alpha Print Company in a suburb north and west of Milwaukee, about 12 miles from her home. To get to work, she ordinarily drives her 1997 Honda Civic. The drive takes her about 25 minutes, depending on the traffic and the weather. She parks in the company parking lot.

On her way to work, Maria drops her daughter off at daycare and her son at Juniper Avenue Elementary School. Her son usually rides home from school with Maria's sister, a third-grade teacher at Juniper; Maria usually picks her daughter up on her way home from work. Sometimes they stop at the grocery store to shop together for dinner.

About one day out of four — the schedule varies from week to week — Maria catches a ride to and from work with her friend Annette, who works at Thanatos Insurance Company near the Alpha Print office. Annette is an accountant, and she does most of her work from her home office, but she goes in to the company office periodically for special meetings. On these days, Annette drops Maria's children off at school and daycare.

When Maria drives to work, she enjoys her second cup of coffee on the road and she listens to taped music from the local Bel Canto Opera Company. She has been practicing for a role in a forthcoming opera with the Bel Canto, and she uses her driving time to get in extra practice. The westbound traffic out of Milwaukee is sometimes bad in the morning, but when Maria gets absorbed in her music she finds that her time on the road passes quickly.

When Maria rides with Annette, she and Annette sometimes pass the time talking about their children and their jobs. But sometimes Maria takes advantage of the opportunity to close her eyes and rest quietly while Annette drives.

Last week Maria's car needed repairs, and Annette was in Chicago. Maria rode a bus to work on Tuesday and Wednesday. On those days she had to make a special arrangement with her sister for getting her children to and from school and daycare. The bus ride required transfers, going and coming, and took about 70 minutes each way. It also required a two-block walk at the end of each ride. Total commuting time for Maria added up to about two-and-a-half hours a day.

Question for Discussion

For Maria, what are the benefits of driving to work rather than riding the bus?

ACTIVITY 10.2

APPROACHES TO REDUCING THE EXTERNAL COSTS OF AUTOMOBILE TRAVEL

Name_____

PART A: TWO PROPOSALS

1. Introduce new systems of congestion-based pricing for the use of selected streets and highways.

What is congestion-based pricing?

Drivers would pay tolls for the use of selected streets and highways, and the tolls would be different for different times of the day. For using streets or highways in certain zones, the toll would be higher at peak traffic times than at other times when traffic is lighter.

What's the idea?

Streets and highways are subject to wide fluctuations in demand. To smooth out the fluctuations and use the streets and highways more efficiently, we could use higher prices to divert some travel to off-peak periods, or to alternate routes.

Has this idea ever been tried?

Yes. Many businesses including movie theaters, airlines and hotels use pricing in this way to encourage business during off-peak times. And governments in Singapore and Hong Kong have used congestion-based pricing to manage traffic flows. In Singapore, congestion-based pricing in certain zones reduced peak-period traffic by about 65 percent.

Wouldn't this require new toll plazas for the roadways in question, introducing a new source of delays?

No. Technology exists today to manage toll systems without the "stop and pay" method that most drivers hate. Cars equipped with on-board transponders are monitored by roadside toll readers and video recorders, and billing is handled by a computerized debit- or credit-card system.

Wouldn't drivers balk at having to pay tolls for roads they now use for free?

Probably, though the roads they use now aren't free. They are paid for by highway taxes. Revenue generated by congestion-based pricing systems could replace or offset existing highway taxes, if legislators devised the law in that way.

2. Convert high-occupancy-vehicle (HOV) lanes to high-occupancy/toll (HOT) lanes.

What is it?

HOV lanes permit vehicles with a certain occupancy rate (say, three or more passengers) to drive on lanes set aside especially for them. Converting these to high-occupancy/toll (HOT) lanes would enable drivers of single-occupancy vehicles to pay a fee and, in return, be permitted to drive in HOV lanes during times when general-occupancy lanes are congested.

ACTIVITY 10.2, CONTINUED

What's the idea?

HOV lanes tend to be underused, often accommodating only about half as many passengers as the adjacent general-use lanes during peak periods. Instead of letting this highway capacity go unused, we could "rent" some of it to drivers of single-occupancy vehicles and thus improve the efficiency of the traffic system.

Has this idea ever been tried?

Yes. On California's State Route 91 tollway, high-occupancy vehicles travel without any toll charges; single-occupancy vehicles pay a toll to use those same lanes. The HOT lanes created in this way ease traffic congestion for the single-occupancy vehicles paying to get into the HOV/HOT lanes and also for the single-occupancy vehicles left behind in the general purpose lanes.

Source: John Semmens, "Buses, Trains, and Automobiles: Finding the Right Transportation Mix for the Phoenix Metro Region." The Goldwater Institute Policy Report No. 188 (January 8, 2004).

PART B: QUESTIONS FOR DISCUSSION

1. Which external costs of automobile travel might be reduced through congestion-based pricing?

   Which ones would be unaffected by congestion-based pricing?

2. Which external costs of automobile travel might be reduced by new systems of HOT lanes?

   Which ones would be unaffected by such new systems?

IF WE GROW MORE FOOD, WON'T WE DEGRADE THE ENVIRONMENT?

LESSON 11

IF WE GROW MORE FOOD, WON'T WE DEGRADE THE ENVIRONMENT?

LESSON DESCRIPTION

The students examine evidence about the impact of modern farming. They analyze the costs and benefits of modern agricultural practices, noting that the benefits derive from improved productivity. They assess the possibility that continued improvements in productivity will soften the environmental impact of modern farming by enabling farmers to produce more food while cultivating less land. To the extent that this occurs, more land will be available for wildlife habitat and recreational activity.

BACKGROUND

Machinery, fertilizers, pesticides, and irrigation systems have been crucial to the development of modern farming. Modern farming has provided a bountiful supply of food, but it also has caused environmental problems, contributing to deforestation, habitat loss, soil erosion, greenhouse gas emissions and water pollution in the United States and elsewhere.

It could be the case that these problems will get worse in the next half-century. World population is expected to grow from 6.3 billion today to about 9 billion by 2050 — an increase of more than 40 percent. Feeding more people will require more food. Producing more food will require expanded, intensified applications of agricultural technology. So we seem to be faced with a tough choice. Should we continue to increase food supplies, at a high cost in environmental impact? Or should we cut back on uses of agricultural technology, at a high cost in food not produced?

Fortunately, that statement of the issue doesn't get things quite right. Despite the environmental problems agricultural technology has caused, technology has also helped to soften agriculture's impact on the environment. Continued innovation in agricultural technology can continue to soften the impact of agriculture, even as the world's farmers boost their output to meet the demands of population growth.

EcoMystery

How can agricultural technology do anything to solve environmental problems caused, in the first place, by agricultural technology?

ECONOMIC REASONING

Technology is an important source of improved productivity. Productivity is output per unit of input.

In agriculture, land is an input. If 30 bushels of wheat are harvested from Acre 1 and 10 bushels are harvested from Acre 2, Acre 1 is three times as productive as Acre 2. What might explain the superior productivity of Acre 1? Planting a high-yield crop variety, perhaps, or perhaps the application of fertilizer or pesticides — in other words, technology.

Improved productivity enables people to produce more goods from a given quantity of inputs. Sometimes improved productivity also enables people to produce more goods from fewer inputs: More newspapers printed by fewer workers, for example, or more wheat grown on fewer acres of land (EcoDetection principle 2).

This potential for obtaining more output from less land (and other inputs) explains why technology may have a mitigating effect on environmental problems caused by agriculture in the next 50 years. Less land required for producing food would mean less deforestation, less soil erosion, less fertilizer run-off into lakes and rivers, and so on (EcoDetection principle 3).

Technology *by itself* could not produce such results. Farmers would need to have access to technology, and they would need to invest in it and use it. Gaining access — the ability to purchase equipment, for example — might require access to credit provided by financial institutions. The choice to invest in technology and use it might be driven by competitive pressures, generated by productive farmers elsewhere.

The potential for using agricultural technology to good environmental effect is likely to be realized, in other words, only in legal and economic environments that provide appropriate incentives for innovation and investment (EcoDetection principle 5).

ECONOMIC CONCEPTS

- Competition
- Incentives
- Private property rights
- Productivity

OBJECTIVES

Students will:

1. Identify environmental problems associated with agriculture.

2. Analyze environmental problems by reference to the concept of *productivity*.

CONTENT STANDARDS

- People respond predictably to positive and negative incentives. (NCEE Content Standard 4.)

- Competition among sellers lowers costs and prices, and encourages producers to produce more of what consumers are willing and able to buy. Competition among buyers increases prices and allocates goods and services to those people willing and able to pay the most for them. (NCEE Content Standard 9.)

- Institutions evolve in market economies to help individuals and groups accomplish their goals. Banks, labor unions, corporations, legal systems, and not-for-profit organizations are examples of important institutions. A different kind of institution, clearly defined and well enforced property rights, is essential to a market economy. (NCEE Content Standard 10.)

- Investment in factories, machinery, new technology, and the health, education, and training of people can raise future standards of living. (NCEE Content Standard 15.)

TIME

60 minutes

MATERIALS

- Classroom set of calculators
- A transparency of Visuals 11.1, 11.2 and 11.3
- A copy of Activities 11.1, 11.2 and 11.3 for each student

PROCEDURE

A. Explain that the purpose of this lesson is to analyze environmental issues related to agriculture. Specifically, the lesson will focus on the relationship between agricultural productivity and environmental protection.

B. **Distribute a copy of Activity 11.1** to each student. Ask the students to read each of the two statements. Discuss each statement briefly, and call on students to respond to the Questions for Discussion.

1. Farming does not go easy on the earth, according to Rauch and Goklany, because the technology it employs destroys habitat, causes water and air pollution, and so on. 2. As more land is converted for use in farming, environmental problems caused by farming will become more widespread. What is already a big problem seems likely to get bigger.

C. The problems summarized by Goklany and Rauch look serious. Ask: Why not try to solve the problems by going back to low-tech farming methods on a broad scale? Why not plow with mules and horses, and pitch hay with pitchforks into those picturesque old haystacks?

It would require big-time coercion to persuade people to leave their office workplaces and go back to the farm — especially if farming meant plowing with horses and mules, milking cows by hand, and so on. And many people would need to be persuaded, since farming would become a very labor-intensive activity. Even if such a transformation could be brought about somehow, food production would go down and food prices would go up.

D. Tell the students that, paradoxically, the solution to the problems summarized by Goklany and Rauch probably will involve more and better uses of technology, not less. That is because technology is an important source of *productivity* in agriculture. **Display Visual 11.1** and discuss the definition of *productivity*.

E. Show the students how technology can be used to increase productivity. In this case, productivity will be measured by the number of problems solved relative to the wage. **Distribute a copy of Activity 11.2** to each student. Begin round one of the demonstration by asking the students to complete as many problems as they can in

Column 1 in two minutes. After two minutes have elapsed, **display Visual 11.2.** Read the answers to the problems in Column 1 to the class. Ask a sample of students how many problems they completed correctly, calculate an average, and record the average on Visual 11.2.

Students, for example, may have completed an average of six problems correctly.

Next, divide the average wage of $1 by the number of problems

For six correct answers: $1 divided by 6 problems = .17 (rounded off).

Record the average cost per correct problem on Visual 11.2.

F. Begin round two. Ask the students to complete as many problems as they can (in Column 2 of Activity 11.2) in two minutes. In this round, however, the students should be allowed to use a calculator. After two minutes, **display Visual 11.2 again.** Read the answers to the problems in Column 2 to the class. Ask a sample of students how many problems they completed correctly, calculate an average, and record the average on Visual 11.2.

Students, for example, may have completed an average of nine problems correctly.

Next, divide the average wage ($1) by the number of problems

For nine correct answers: $1 divided by 9 problems = .11.

Record the average cost per correct problem.

G. Discuss the results of the demonstration. Students should note that introducing technology by the use of calculators made them more productive in solving mathematics problems correctly. They produced more correct answers in the time available. The cost of solving problems declined. Invite the students to speculate on other ways in which they could increase their productivity in solving problems.

H. What does this have to do with agriculture and the environment? Explain that technology has helped farmers produce food in the same way it helped students solve problems. With productivity enhanced by technology, farmers have been able to produce food in ample quantities. But that

is not the only beneficial result. **Distribute a copy of Activity 11.3** to each student. Discuss the two statements and the students' responses to the questions. Emphasize the main point: Advances in agricultural technology have enabled farmers to produce more food using less land than otherwise would have been required. Keeping land out of agricultural production has softened the impact of agricultural technology to date.

I. What about the future? Can we expect to see more gains in agricultural productivity, enabling us to avoid conversion of prime habitat into farmland, or have we gone about as far as we can go in that direction? It is a big question. To illustrate the possibilities and the uncertainties, introduce an innovation called no-till farming. **Display Visual 11.3.** Discuss no-till farming and its relationship to genetic engineering in agriculture. Underscore the dilemma: an innovation that might improve agricultural productivity in an earth-friendly way raises fears and stirs up resistance because it depends on new technology that is as yet imperfectly understood.

J. To conclude, tell the students that the point of the lesson is not to take sides at the moment on any specifics in the controversy surrounding applications of genetic technology in agriculture. Instead, the brief account of no-till farming and its link to genetic engineering illustrates one recent development in an ongoing search for innovations designed to improve agricultural productivity and thus reduce the amount of land needed for raising food. The search for innovations is not merely a matter of science or technology. It may be encouraged or discouraged by the legal and economic environment in which farmers, researchers, and consumers go about their business. Ask: Which of the following conditions would help to establish an environment in which innovation is encouraged? The students should explain their answers by reference to principles of EcoDetection.

- Owners of retail food markets are free to decide what products they will sell. They may sell only organic or "natural" foods, certified to contain no genetically modified ingredients. These foods will be relatively expensive. Or they may sell a wider range of foods, more variously priced, including foods not labeled as organic or "natural." Some of these foods will contain genetically modified ingredients. Consumers are free to shop at the natural foods markets or at other markets.

This condition would encourage innovation. Producers and retailers of each variety of food would have an incentive to satisfy consumers. Nobody would continue to produce or sell food varieties rejected by consumers.

- The income farmers earn is determined largely by subsidy payments from the government. These payments have nothing to do with productivity. Farmers who produce less food using more inputs receive subsidies on the same scale as those who are much more productive.

This condition would not encourage innovation. Less productive farmers would have no strong incentive to compete with more productive ones by figuring out how to grow more food using fewer inputs.

- Biotechnology researchers who develop new products through genetic engineering obtain legal ownership of those products through patents or copyrights. If these products prove to be commercially successful, the researchers who develop them will earn a share of the profits.

This condition would encourage innovation. The opportunity to earn a profit would create an incentive for researchers to do their work well.

Closure

Review the key points of the lesson by reference to the concepts of *productivity, competition, incentives* and *private property rights.*

- Productivity: Improvements in productivity enable farmers to produce more food and cut costs while using fewer inputs, including less land under cultivation. Less land under cultivation may mean more land preserved for wildlife habitat and recreation.

- In a competitive agricultural market, farmers have an incentive to improve productivity through innovation.

- The incentive to innovate and compete depends upon an underlying legal structure that permits people to own property — ideas as well as land and objects. The prospect of earning a profit from a

patent on a biotech product encourages researchers to pursue research; the prospect of earning a profit from a high-yield, no-till farm encourages farmers to pursue farming in that way.

Assessment

Multiple-Choice Questions

1. Productivity refers to the
   a. average level of prices over a period of time.
   b. output per unit of input.
   c. average output per worker during a given period of time.
   d. total level of prices over a period of time.

2. Which of the following best describes the relationship between agricultural productivity and environmental degradation?
   a. The technology used to improve agricultural productivity destroys the environment.
   b. The technology used to improve agricultural productivity prevents environmental problems from arising.
   c. The technology used to improve agricultural productivity requires more land to be brought under cultivation.
   d. The technology used to improve agricultural productivity decreases the amount of land that must be brought under cultivation.

Essay Questions

1. How do economic incentives affect food production and environmental protection? Explain your answer.

Economic incentives encourage farmers to be productive. Farmers who want to be productive innovate, using new technologies. Technology has increased farm yields, but it also has caused environmental problems. At the same time, technology has made it possible for farmers to produce more food using less land. Using less land for farming has meant less deforestation, less fertilizer runoff and less soil erosion. Ongoing innovations in agriculture including no-till farming and genetic engineering may improve productivity further. If they do, the amount of land devoted to agriculture may be further reduced and the amount available for habitat and recreation may be increased accordingly.

2. Respond to the following statement:

"Environmental problems related to farming are basically technical problems: Some fertilizers cause harmful runoff, some pesticides have toxic effects on wildlife, and some methods of plowing cause soil erosion — the list goes on and on. These are problems that require technical solutions. The politicians and lawyers should keep their noses out of this area. They don't have the technical expertise we need in order to make progress in solving environmental problems related to farming."

Politicians and lawyers often do make things worse by supporting bad policies. Still, it isn't enough merely to rely on improved, Earth-friendly technology as a source of solutions for environmental problems related to farming. No matter how brilliant they may be, technical innovations in farming don't achieve anything unless they are put to use by farmers. In deciding whether to make use of an innovation, a farmer will consider costs and benefits. If farmers must invest in new equipment to use the innovation, they may need to borrow money. They are unlikely to borrow money — and bankers will be unlikely to lend it — unless they think they can earn a profit by using the new equipment. Earth-friendly effects of new technology in farming depend, in other words, on an underlying economic and legal system that encourages farmers to seek profits through innovation and investment.

VISUAL 11.1

PRODUCTIVITY

- Definition: Productivity is output per unit of input.

- Role of technology: Technological advancements are an important source of productivity. Many inventions have increased productivity, including the steam engine, the internal combustion engine and computers.

- What happens when productivity increases? People can produce more goods from a given quantity of inputs, or more goods from fewer inputs.

VISUAL 11.2

WHAT DOES A CORRECT ANSWER TO A PROBLEM COST?

Round	Wage	Average Number Correct	Average Cost Per Problem
1	$1.00		
2	$1.00		

VISUAL 11.3

NO-TILL FARMING AND GENETICALLY-MODIFIED CROPS

- For thousands of years, farmers have plowed their fields, often several times per year.

- Plowing causes runoff from fields — eroding adjacent land, polluting rivers and releasing greenhouse gases from the soil into the atmosphere. Also, soil plowed repeatedly becomes lifeless.

- Today many American farmers are experimenting with no-till farming. This means they don't plow their fields.

- One such experiment near Richmond, Virginia, has produced topsoil rich in organic matter, without any chemical or soil runoff. Because this soil has not been plowed, it produces an underground ecosystem of insects, roots and micro-organisms. That ecosystem holds the earth in place and becomes a sponge for water. No-till farmers in this area get excellent crop yields, create no erosion and save money they otherwise would have spent on fuel used to power tractors pulling plows.

- Is there any downside to no-till farming? Maybe. Maybe not. Widespread elimination of plowing depends on genetically-modified crops. That is because weeds grow rapidly in fields that don't get plowed — unless herbicides are applied to kill the weeds. To cope with this problem, no-till farmers use crop varieties genetically engineered to tolerate special herbicides that can be applied in small quantities. More than a third of all U.S. soybeans are now grown without plowing and with reduced applications of herbicides — mostly thanks to genetic engineering.

VISUAL 11.3, CONTINUED

- Genetically-modified crops are highly controversial, especially in England and Europe. Critics fear that organisms produced by genetic engineering may spread from fields to other areas, causing a nuisance or worse, or that engineered plants might cross-pollinate with neighboring plants, producing invasive "superweeds." Environmentalists generally have resisted genetic engineering in agriculture, therefore, despite its potential to foster no-till farming and other environmentally friendly innovations.

Source: Jonathan Rauch, "Will Frankenfood Save the Planet?" The Atlantic Monthly (October 2003).

ACTIVITY 11.1

FARMING DOES NOT GO EASY ON THE EARTH

Name_____

Read the two statements below; then respond to the Questions for Discussion.

1. Worldwide, agriculture accounts for 38 percent of land use, 66 percent of water withdrawals and 85 percent of water consumption. It is responsible for most of the habitat loss and fragmentation that threaten the world's forests, biodiversity, and terrestrial carbon stores and sinks. Water diversions for agriculture combined with agriculture-related water quality problems (oxygen depletion, pesticide and fertilizer runoff, and soil erosion) are the major threats to aquatic and avian species not only inland but, possibly, also in coastal and nearshore areas. In addition, land clearance and other agricultural practices contribute to greenhouse gas emissions.

Source: Indur M. Goklany, "The Pros and Cons of Modern Farming," PERC Reports 19 (March 2001).

2. It is only a modest exaggeration to say that as goes agriculture, so goes the planet. Of all the human activities that shape the environment, agriculture is the single most important…Today about 38 percent of the earth's land area is cropland or pasture — a total that has crept up over the past few decades as global population has grown. The increase has been gradual, only about 3 percent a year; but that still translates into an additional Greece or Nicaragua cultivated or grazed every year.

Farming does not go easy on the earth… To farm is to make war upon millions of plants (weeds, so-called) and animals (pests, so called) that in the ordinary course of things would crowd out or eat or infest whatever it is the farmer is growing. Crop monocultures, as whole fields of… wheat or corn or any other single plant are called, make poor habitat and are vulnerable to disease and disaster. Although fertilizer runs off and pollutes water, farming without fertilizer will deplete and eventually exhaust the soil. Pesticides can harm the health of human beings and kill desirable bugs along with pests. Irrigation leaves behind trace elements that can accumulate and poison the soil. And so on.

Source: Jonathan Rauch, "Will Frankenfood Save the Planet?" The Atlantic Monthly (October 2003).

Questions for Discussion

1. What does Rauch mean by his statement that "farming does not go easy on the earth"?

2. Goklany refers to land clearance as a problem; Rauch, similarly writes of an annual increase in land area devoted to farming. What is problematic about this increase?

ACTIVITY 11.2

MATHEMATICS PROBLEMS

Name_____

You will be given two minutes per work period to complete the problems below. Try to answer correctly as many problems as possible in the time limit. Wait for your teacher's instructions before beginning.

	Column 1		Column 2
1.	48 + 55 =	1.	23 + 38 =
2.	34 + 88 - 9 =	2.	55 + 19 - 4 =
3.	12 x 30 =	3.	14 x 50 =
4.	15 x 25 =	4.	17 x 25 =
5.	43 x 22 =	5.	33 x 12 =
6.	587 ÷ 12 =	6.	754 ÷ 12 =
7.	360 ÷ 50 =	7.	817 ÷ 30 =
8.	655 ÷ 50 =	8.	255 ÷ 20 =
9.	(5 x 16) + (80 x 16) =	9.	(3 x 13) + (60 x 15) =
10.	(7 x 10) + (8 x 9) =	10.	(9 x 4) + (4 x 11) =

ACTIVITY 11.3

TECHNOLOGY, PRODUCTIVITY AND LAND USE:
HOW IMPORTANT IS THE LAND THAT DIDN'T GET FARMED?

Name_____

Read the statements below; then respond to the Questions for Discussion.

1. Paradoxically, agricultural technology is…responsible for forestalling [Rachel Carson's dreaded] silent springs — at least so far. Had technology — and therefore [farm] yields — been frozen [over the last several years] at 1961 levels, then producing as much food as was actually produced in 1998 would have required more than a doubling of land devoted to agriculture. Such land would have increased from 12.2 billion acres to at least 26.3 billion acres, that is, from 38 to 82 percent of global land area…Cropland alone would have had to more than double, from 3.7 to 7.9 billion acres. [It would have been necessary to plow under] an additional area the size of South America minus Chile.…

Imagine the devastation that would have occurred…while [human] mortality rates continued to drop, pushing up population. Massive deforestation, soil erosion, greenhouse gas emissions, and losses of biodiversity would occur with the more-than-doubling of land and water diverted to agriculture, but hunger and starvation would not [have declined]. The additional pressure on the land would have increased land prices, making it more difficult to reserve land for conservation.…

Such tragic results did not happen, thanks to improvements in productivity at each step of the…agricultural system.

Source: Indur M Goklany, "The Pros and Cons of Modern Farming," PERC Reports 19 (March 2001).

2. One reason to improve [agricultural] yields even further through new means such as biotechnology is to keep uncultivated or wild lands from production. For much of the last half-century, that has been the true accomplishment of increased yields. The question was not whether we would have enough food for everyone, but how much land we would have to plow to [produce] the necessary food.

Norman Borlaug, who won the 1970 Nobel prize for increasing grain yields worldwide, explains this achievement. According to Borlaug…, [it would have been necessary to cultivate] an additional 850 million hectares (2.1 billion acres) of land…to equal [the 1999] cereal harvest if we [had] used 1961 technology [to do so]. Jesse Ausubel…of Rockefeller University estimates that if the world's average farmer reaches the yield of the average (not the best!) U.S. corn grower, it will take only half of today's current cropland to feed [an estimated 9 billion people in the future].

Source: J. Bishop Grewell, Farming for the Future: Agriculture's Next Generation (Bozeman, Montana: PERC, 2002), pp. 7-8.

Questions for Discussion

1. According to Goklany and Grewell, what is the relationship between improved productivity and land use?

2. According to Goklany and Grewell, what are some environmental effects of using less land for farming?

RECYCLING OR LANDFILL DISPOSAL: WHAT IS THE BEST WAY TO PROTECT THE ENVIRONMENT?

LESSON 12

RECYCLING OR LANDFILL DISPOSAL: WHAT IS THE BEST WAY TO PROTECT THE ENVIRONMENT?

LESSON DESCRIPTION

The students investigate four proposed recycling programs (curbside recycling, newspaper recycling, recycling of aluminum cans, and banning disposable diapers from landfills) and decide whether the programs should be adopted or not. They use principles of economic reasoning to defend their positions and explain positions held by others.

BACKGROUND

Recycling has always provided a way to deal with some waste products. Farmers have recycled manure as fertilizer, and fashionistas have made vital fashion statements thanks to vintage clothing they purchase in boutique resale shops. About 20 years ago, however, recycling began to take priority over traditional means of waste disposal for a wide range of waste materials. Public demands, governmental subsidies and mandated recycling programs contributed to development of the extensive recycling programs that now exist in most communities.

The recycling movement has been driven by a widespread belief that recycling is an environmentally friendly practice. This belief encourages many individuals to recycle. It also serves as a basis for government policies designed to encourage or require households to recycle household trash and garbage. Economists like to point out, however, that recycling policies can be misguided. **Some garbage is not worth recycling because recycling in some cases uses more resources than the resources conserved by the recycling process.**

Recycling is an industrial process. It requires the use of land, labor, capital and energy to convert discarded products into useable resources. And the recycling process itself creates waste products. This observation is not to suggest that recycling in general is a misguided idea. Recycling is the right thing to do when the benefits of recycling outweigh the costs. But when recycling costs exceed benefits, resources are wasted. The environment is not protected by programs that waste resources.

EcoMystery

Protecting the environment involves using resources carefully. Yet some recycling programs waste resources. Why would people concerned about environmental protection defend a practice that wastes resources?

ECONOMIC REASONING

Most people see recycling as an environmentally friendly practice by means of which garbage gets converted into useful resources, thus reducing the amount of waste material going to landfills. This belief prompts many individuals to recycle cans, bottles, paper, plastics and cardboard into separate containers. It also prompts policy makers to establish curbside recycling programs (EcoDetection principle 5). Unfortunately, it does not require anybody to consider the costs of recycling. Some recycled items like aluminum and steel are very valuable to producers. Businesses will pay enough for these items to cover the costs involved. Other materials like plastics and newspaper are less valuable to producers, and nobody will pay enough for them to cover recycling costs (EcoDetection principle 2).

To an economist, it is an efficient use of resources to recycle materials when the costs of recycling are covered by the price people will pay for the recycled materials. It is an inefficient (wasteful) use of resources to recycle materials when the costs of recycling are greater than the price people will pay for them.

ECONOMIC CONCEPTS

- Benefit
- Choice
- Cost
- Incentives

OBJECTIVES

Students will:

1. Investigate the costs and benefits of recycling programs.

2. Evaluate recycling programs by reference to principles of economic reasoning.

3. Explain how incentives influence people in their decisions about recycling.

CONTENT STANDARDS

- People respond predictably to positive and negative incentives. (NCEE Content Standard 4.)

- There is an economic role for government to play in a market economy whenever the benefits of a government policy outweigh its costs. Governments often provide for national defense, address environmental concerns, define and protect property rights, and attempt to make markets more competitive. Most government policies also redistribute income. (NCEE Content Standard 16.)

- Costs of government policies sometimes exceed benefits. This may occur because of incentives facing voters, government officials, and government employees, because of actions by special interest groups that can impose costs on the general public, or because social goals other than economic efficiency are being pursued. (NCEE Content Standard 17.)

TIME

60 minutes

MATERIALS

- A transparency of Visuals 12.1

- A copy of Activities 12.1, 12.2, 12.3 and 12.4 for each student

- Optional background reading for the teacher: Daniel K. Benjamin, "Eight Great Myths of Recycling" (PERC, 2003). Available at www.perc.org.

PROCEDURE

A. Explain to the students that in this lesson they will investigate an issue that is rarely thought of as controversial. That issue is recycling. Recycling has the status of something like a sacred cow among many people who seek to protect the environment. Is that status well deserved? What do we actually know about how well recycling serves the cause of environmental protection?

B. Display typical household waste materials. Include a newspaper, an aluminum can, a plastic bottle, a piece of cardboard, some used facial tissue, some cardboard, food wrappers and a disposable diaper (a clean one, of course).

C. Ask the students which of these items can be recycled into useable materials.

Typically, students will select the newspaper, the aluminum can, the plastic bottle and the cardboard. The correct answer, in fact, is all of them. Any waste material can be recycled if one wishes to do so.

D. Ask the students to identify several of the many things we reuse and recycle every day — such as clothes, dishes, automobiles, textbooks, DVDs, even paintings. Let them brainstorm about the possibilities so they can see that reusing and recycling items is a widespread, voluntary activity.

E. Anything can be recycled, but in fact people tend to recycle some things and not others. They must have some basis for making these decisions. Ask: Of all the things that can be recycled, how do we decide what we will recycle?

Answers are likely to vary. Offer clues as necessary to encourage answers based on the concepts of costs and benefits: Recycling is an efficient practice in cases in which the benefits of recycling exceed the costs.

F. **Distribute a copy of Activity 12.1** to each student. Divide the class into groups of three or four students. Assign the students to read the four proposals, discuss them in their groups, and, making use of the principles of EcoDetection, respond to the Questions for Discussion.

Responses are apt to vary greatly. Students often support recycling and express strong feelings about this subject. Depending on priorities and other constraints, teachers may wish to extend the time allocated for the presentation and discussion of the groups' responses. The discussion could include consideration of Daniel K. Benjamin's "Eight Great Myths of Recycling," cited in the Materials list. It might also be useful to invite a local recycling official into the classroom to discuss Benjamin's arguments so that both sides of the issue are presented to the students.

G. **Distribute a copy of Activity 12.2** to each student. Explain that different people can look at the same issue and the same information and reach different conclusions. One reason for this variability in responses is that different people are influenced by different incentives. Assign the students to read Activity 12.2 and identify the incentives that seem to influence the thinking of Rudman, Farr, and Brie.

Rudman

- *Position: Favors the curbside recycling program.*

- *Incentives: Accomplish his goals; retain his job; resources do not come from his office, so someone else bears most of the project's cost. Environmental protection has little to do with his position.*

Farr

- *Position: Favors the curbside recycling program.*

- *Incentives: Convenience; major costs are borne by someone else. The overall impact on the environment does not enter into her decision.*

Brie

- *Position: Opposes the curbside recycling program*

- *Incentives: Cost; his company and his budget must bear significant costs of the recycling program. The company makes a small return for selling cans, but the returns do not cover the cost of extra trucks and workers. Environmental protection does not enter into Brie's decision except in respect to the waste caused because more people and equipment are needed to do the same amount of work.*

H. **Distribute a copy of Activity 12.3** to each student. Ask the students to take the Recycling Quiz. Discuss their responses.

I. **Distribute a copy of Activity 12.4** to each student. Discuss the answers to the quiz and compare them to the students' initial responses.

J. **Display Visual 12.1.** Ask the students to solve the mystery.

They should note that people's choices regarding recycling do influence environmental quality. Recycling, however, involves costs. People will voluntarily choose to recycle when the personal costs are low. When the personal costs are high, they prefer to place material into landfills and use the savings for other worthwhile purposes. People will support recycling when it costs them little or when the costs of recycling can be passed on to other people.

CLOSURE

Review the main points of the lesson. Ask:

- Do people recycle voluntarily?

Yes. Many companies make profits or reduce their costs by recycling paper, glass, aluminum, tires and oil. Many individuals recycle their cars, toys, clothes and books by donating them to thrift stores.

- Under what circumstances would you expect to see more voluntary recycling?

Voluntary recycling increases when prices are high for recycled materials or when new technology enables recycling companies to make profits even when prices are low.

- Under what circumstances might people choose not to recycle?

If the cost of recycling is too high or recycling is inconvenient. People might then decide to place some materials in the garbage for the landfill and use their resources for other purposes.

- Under what circumstances will policy makers create a recycling program that wastes resources?

When they lack the information about the waste involved or when other people are required to bear the costs of the wasteful activity.

ASSESSMENT

Multiple-Choice Questions

1. Many companies recycle glass, aluminum, tires and steel because they wish to

   a. earn a profit.

   b. fight city hall.

   c. claim a tax deduction.

   d. avoid competition.

2. Which of the following items is the least likely to be recycled?

   a. A steel can

   b. An aluminum can

   c. An automobile

   d. Used medical instruments

Essay Questions

1. Respond to the following statement, making use of the principles of EcoDetection.

"People are ignorant and stubborn by nature. Everyone knows that recycling is important for protecting the environment, yet people still throw plastic bottles and newspapers into the garbage. How do you explain that behavior?"

People respond to incentives. Sometimes it is very inconvenient to recycle newspaper. It has to be stored, wrapped and delivered. Some people have better things to do with their time and storage space. In addition, they may know that newspaper recycling causes other major environmental problems like disposing of ink sludge and using large amounts of water. Therefore, they may decide it is better for the environment if they do not recycle newspapers.

2. Should citizens be encouraged to recycle materials? Economists have pointed out that there are many cases in which recycling wastes resources.

People should be encouraged to recycle when recycling is helpful to the environment. Economists would favor recycling when the benefits of recycling are greater than the costs of recycling. Recycling old automobiles, human blood, and aluminum cans usually meets this standard. But people should be discouraged from recycling items when the costs of recycling are greater than the benefits.

LESSON 12

VISUAL 12.1

THE MYSTERY OF RECYCLING PROGRAMS GONE BAD

Protecting the environment involves using resources carefully. Yet some recycling programs waste resources. Why would people who are concerned about environmental protection defend a practice that wastes resources?

ACTIVITY 12.1

FOUR RECYCLING PROPOSALS

Name_____

Imagine that you are a committed citizen who wants to be a good environmental steward. You are also familiar with the principles of EcoDetection. So you become interested when you find out that your community council is considering four different proposals to encourage recycling. Each proposal is described below. Short statements pro and con are provided as well. Read the proposals and respond to the Questions for Discussion.

PROPOSAL A: CURBSIDE RECYCLING

This proposal would require the local garbage collection firm to create a curbside recycling program. The company would have to provide home owners with four different recycling bins for plastic, newspapers, glass and metal cans. Home owners would sort their recyclable material into the four appropriate bins and put them by the curb for pick-up once a week. The company would have to purchase trucks and hire workers to travel through the neighborhood five days a week to pick up the recycled materials. The company would be allowed to sell all the recycled materials.

> **Pro:** This proposal would reduce the amount of garbage that is sent to the landfill. Right now the landfill is on track to be full in 30 years. This proposal would extend that period to 45 years. It would also reduce the amount of raw resources like petroleum, electrical energy, trees, sand and bauxite needed to make newspapers, aluminum cans, plastics and glass. The revenue from selling the recycled materials would provide the company with additional money to recover some of its costs.

> **Con:** This proposal wastes resources. It doubles the number of waste-disposal trucks in the collection company's fleet, and it doubles the number of collection trucks used in the neighborhood. Consider how many resources are necessary to build those trucks, the gasoline necessary to fuel those trucks, and the additional air pollution created by the additional trucks. All this consumption of resources and new pollution could be avoided by not requiring curbside recycling. Also, the material to be recycled here would produce almost no new revenue. Only the metal (aluminum) cans could be sold. The other materials have little or no market value. In fact, recycling companies often pay waste-disposal companies to take plastics and glass to a landfill site.

PROPOSAL B: NEWSPAPER RECYCLING

This proposal would require local residents to recycle all their newspapers by taking them to a collection site where the city employees would collect them and sell them to paper recyclers. Newspapers would no longer be permitted in the household garbage picked up by the waste-disposal company.

> **Pro:** Recycling newspapers would reduce the amount of garbage thrown into the local landfill. It would reduce the total amount of garbage collected by the waste disposal company, making it easier for the company to do its job quickly and efficiently. Paper recycling would also save trees and prevent deforestation by reducing the demand for paper made from trees.

> **Con:** Recycling newspapers is an industrial process that creates as much pollution and requires the use of as many resources as making paper from trees. Newspaper recycling requires tons of water to wash the paper, plus bleaches to make it appear clean. This process creates large amounts of sludge, which is sometimes toxic. The sludge must be dumped in a toxic-waste dump. Most paper is made from trees

LESSON 12

ACTIVITY 12.1, CONTINUED

grown on tree farms specifically intended to supply paper mills. No one uses old-growth trees for paper production. If demand for trees declines because trees cannot be used for paper, people will produce fewer trees. Recycling paper does not save trees, and it adds to pollution and resource-use problems.

PROPOSAL C: RECYCLE METAL CANS

This proposal calls on citizens to save all their aluminum and steel cans and drop them off at a convenient recycling center where they would be paid for the cans. The city would sell the cans to aluminum and steel producers for the going market price. The program would continue as long as the city received a higher sale price for the recycled materials than it paid out to citizens for the cans.

> **Pro:** Aluminum and steel cans can be easily converted into reusable metals. Recycled aluminum and steel are cheaper to acquire and easier to use in the manufacturing process; thus aluminum and steel producers are paying relatively high prices for these materials. Recycling these materials also reduces the amount of new ore that has to be mined to create aluminum and steel.

> **Con:** There is no need to recycle these materials because the world is not running out of iron ore and bauxite, the metals that are used to create steel and aluminum. Prices for recycled aluminum and steel change every day, so the city might not be able to get a price that covers the cost of collecting these materials and paying the citizens.

PROPOSAL D: BAN DISPOSABLE DIAPERS.

This proposal would ban disposable diapers as components of municipal waste; it would require citizens to dispose of disposable diapers in a separate facility — or use reusable diapers (the original recycling plan for diapers).

> **Pro:** The *New York Times* has called disposable diapers a "symbol of the nation's garbage crisis," and the *Portland Oregonian* has reported that disposable diapers make up one quarter of the contents of the Portland-area landfills. These unsanitary items should be excluded from the landfills to prevent water contamination, promote public health standards and reduce the amount of municipal waste going to landfills.

> **Con:** Disposable diapers are a convenience for busy people with small children. They actually take up one percent of landfill space, and landfill space is abundant and increasing in the United States. New landfills must now be built so that they prevent all leakage into ground water. Washing reusable diapers contributes to sewage problems that must be corrected with water-treatment plants. Washing reusable diapers also requires large amounts of hot water (heated by electricity created by fossil fuels) and soap.

ACTIVITY 12.1, CONTINUED

Questions for Discussion

1. Which recycling program(s) would you support?

2. Which principles of EcoDetection support your position?

3. Write a short paragraph explaining your position on the recycling program(s) you support. Be sure to use one or more principles of EcoDetection in explaining your position.

LESSON 12

ACTIVITY 12.2

POSITIONS ON RECYCLING PROGRAMS

Name_____

Below are statements by three different people about a curbside recycling proposal. It is the same proposal described in Activity 12.1 — the proposal that probably will not save any resources. Yet people hold various opinions of it. Read their statements and see if you can identify the incentives that influence their thinking in each case.

Richard Rudman I'm the manager of the city recycling program. My department is held accountable for its work, and I agree with that requirement. We are supposed to increase the amount of household municipal waste that is recycled, and the curbside recycling program will help us accomplish that goal. Curbside recycling is convenient. People don't have to use their cars to carry materials to a central location. Just take it out to the street once a week. I know it is an expensive program, but recycling is good for the environment and it will help me do my job better.

• Position: _____

• Incentives: _____

Tawnya Farr I'm an average citizen working as a cashier at Big Box Merchandise Store. It is important to protect the environment. I don't have the time or money it would take to travel to Brazil to try to save the rain forest or to help create habitat for endangered species. I do have time and interest enough to recycle my household garbage, which I have been taught to believe is good for the environment. The convenience of curbside recycling is very important to me. I don't understand why people think it is too expensive. It doesn't cost me anything. The waste disposal company has to provide all the trucks and workers to move the stuff. Cost is their problem, not mine.

• Position: _____

• Incentives: _____

Stan Brie I'm the local manager for Waste Disposal, Inc. in this community. To make this curbside program work, I have to buy an additional 100 trucks and hire an additional 100 people. In the end we will move just as much municipal waste as we did before, but now I need to hire additional people and equipment so I can deliver some garbage to the landfill and some recyclables to a recycling center. That decision seems to be a waste of resources to me and my boss. It's also going to leave another messy problem for us. I can sell the cans for a small amount, but where do we store the glass, cardboard and plastic that no one wants? We can't sell it and we don't have any place to store it. I may have to pay someone to take it away and throw it in some other landfill.

• Position: _____

• Incentives: _____

ACTIVITY 12.3

RECYCLING QUIZ

Name_____

Mark each statement below true (T) or false (F), according to the discussion in your group.
Then discuss your responses with the class.

1. Some businesses voluntarily buy material that can be recycled. _____

2. Recycling happens only because it is required by law. _____

3. Nearly anything can be recycled. _____

4. Recycling always saves resources. _____

5. Recyclable materials are usually placed in landfills because of people's ignorance about what is good for the environment. _____

ACTIVITY 12.4

ANSWERS TO THE RECYCLING QUIZ

Name_____

1. Some businesses voluntarily buy material that can be recycled. _____

   True. Some well-established businesses specialize in recycling paper, aluminum, steel and automobile parts.

2. Recycling happens only because it is required by law. _____

   False. The vast majority of recycling occurs voluntarily. Businesses have been involved in recycling for many years because recycling is profitable. Even before curbside recycling, people often recycled newspapers through newspaper drives. More and more aluminum cans are recycled because it is often cheaper to use recycled aluminum than to produce new aluminum. Car parts are routinely recycled, as are human hearts, eyes, kidneys and blood.

3. Nearly anything can be recycled. _____

   True. The increased price of some recyclable materials has encouraged the development of new technologies for recycling. Nearly all materials can be recycled using super-hot furnaces that break waste down into molecules and atoms. The more important question is this: How much does it cost to recycle particular materials relative to the sought-after benefits of producing more materials from original resources?

4. Recycling always saves resources. _____

   False. Whether recycling saves resources depends on the cost of recycling and the technology involved. Plastic containers, for example, require less energy to produce for one-time use than do containers made from glass or aluminum. Newspapers are very expensive to recycle and create a serious problem of disposal for the ink sludge (which is sometimes toxic) created in the recycling process.

5. Recyclable materials are usually placed in landfills because of people's ignorance about what is good for the environment. _____

   False. Often recyclable materials are placed in landfills because the cost of other alternatives is too high. When prices for newsprint and plastic rise, recycling centers take in these materials, transform them and resell them. When the prices for newsprint and plastic fall, recycling centers will send the materials to the landfill.

FOREST FIRES: NATURAL CATASTROPHES OR MONSTERS WE HAVE CREATED?

LESSON 13

FOREST FIRES: NATURAL CATASTROPHES OR MONSTERS WE HAVE CREATED?

LESSON DESCRIPTION

The students examine information about the ongoing threat of catastrophic fires facing many forests in the United States, especially national forests in the West. They analyze possible explanations for the threat posed by fires and use economic reasoning to assess the explanations.

BACKGROUND

By some measures, America's forests today are abundant and productive. The number of wooded acres in the United States has grown by 20 percent since about 1970. Average annual wood growth in the United States is now three times what it was in 1920. In the four states of Maine, New Hampshire, Vermont and New York, there are 26 million more acres of forest land today than there were at the turn of the century. Increasingly abundant forests have supported population growth for some species of wildlife once thought to be endangered, including the timber wolf and the bald eagle. Forests also have supported an important industry. The United States today is a major supplier of commercial wood, accounting for one fourth of the world's total output.

This portrait of abundance and productivity reflects the strong interest Americans have in healthy forests. We depend on forests for trees, of course. But healthy forests supply many byproducts that we also value, including clean water, clean air, wildlife habitat and various recreational opportunities. Accordingly, the guiding philosophy of our public agencies is to preserve wilderness, biodiversity and landscape beauty as well as to protect soil, water and air quality. These goals are supported by appropriations from Congress of hundreds of millions of dollars each year.

Against this encouraging background, one troublesome fact stands out. Our national forests, especially those in the Western states, have been ravaged in recent years by destructive wildfires. In 2000, 7.5 million acres burned — an area roughly the size of Massachusetts, Rhode Island and Delaware combined. In 2002, nearly 7 million acres burned. The Forest Service predicts more bad

fires in the future. It estimates that 190 million acres of federal forests and rangelands — an area twice the size of California — face a high, ongoing risk of catastrophic fire.

ECOMYSTERY

Nobody wants to see wildfires devastate forests. But devastation from fire is a very real threat for many forests today, especially our national forests in the West. How has the threat of catastrophic fires come about?

ECONOMIC REASONING

Wildfires arise from many causes, including drought, lightning strikes and human carelessness. But for many publicly owned Western forests, the threat posed by these sources has been heightened by government policies and regulations (EcoDetection principle 5). Congressional funding formulas have created an incentive for the U.S. Forest Service to emphasize fire suppression as a top priority (EcoDetection principle 4). A long history of fire suppression has deprived forests of the benefits that frequent, low-intensity fires once provided. Also, regulatory constraints have imposed stringent limits on timber cutting on public lands. The combined effect of fire suppression and decreased timber cutting has been to leave vast forest areas overgrown and cluttered with dead wood and brush. The buildup of "fuel loads" on forest floors creates ideal conditions for the ignition of fires, especially during droughts (EcoDetection principle 3). And densely crowded tree tops provide avenues along which fires (called crown fires) can spread rapidly, fanned at tree-top height by the wind.

Many forest ecologists recommend programs of active management to reduce these risks, and the Forest Service now endorses forest thinning and timber sales as components of its approach to forest restoration through active management. But it remains to be seen whether the Forest Service will be able to develop and implement this approach extensively. Congressional funding of the Forest Service creates an incentive for continued emphasis on fire suppression, and the regulatory climate still stands as an obstacle to timber sales.

By contrast, privately owned forests typically are actively managed — thinned, selectively harvested and made suitable for multiple uses, depending on demand for timber, recreational sites and wildlife habitat. Private landowners are motivated by a desire to protect the commercial value of their property (EcoDetection principle 6), and they face fewer regulatory constraints than those faced by Forest Service managers.

ECONOMIC CONCEPTS

- Incentives
- Private property ownership
- Profits

OBJECTIVES

Students will:

1. Analyze forest-management practices of private landowners by reference to incentives.

2. Analyze forest-management practices of the U.S. Forest Service by reference to incentives.

3. Evaluate proposed initiatives aimed at changing the incentives that shape forest-management practices.

CONTENT STANDARDS

- Productive resources are limited. Therefore, people cannot have all the goods and services they want; as a result, they must choose some things and give up others. (NCEE Content Standard 1.)

- People respond predictably to positive and negative incentives. (NCEE Content Standard 4.)

- There is an economic role for government to play in a market economy whenever the benefits of a government policy outweigh its costs. Governments often provide for national defense, address environmental concerns, define and protect property rights, and attempt to make markets more competitive. Most government policies also redistribute income. (NCEE Content Standard 16.)

- Costs of government policies sometimes exceed benefits. This may occur because of incentives facing voters, government officials, and government employees, because of actions by special interest groups that can impose costs on the general public, or because social goals other than economic efficiency are being pursued. (NCEE Content Standard 17.)

TIME

75 minutes

MATERIALS

- A transparency of Visuals 13.1, 13.2, 13.3 and 13.4
- A copy of Activities 13.1, 13.2 and 13.3 for each student

PROCEDURE

A. Explain to the students that in this lesson they will explore issues related to the wildfires that have recently caused widespread destruction in our national forests, especially in the Western states.

B. Ask the students to respond — individually, briefly, and in writing — to this question: What do you suppose the condition of America's forests is today, across the nation? (Students may object that this is a very general question; forest conditions probably vary from place to place, etc. Acknowledge the validity of these points, but tell the students you would like nonetheless to have them put down their best estimate of forest conditions generally.) When the students have recorded their responses, move on, without discussion, to Procedure C.

C. **Display Visual 13.1.** Call on volunteers to read the Visual. Discuss the main points briefly. Then ask the students to turn to the notes they wrote in response to your question from Procedure B. Ask them to contrast the information shown on the Visual with the notes they wrote.

   The students' responses to the question from Procedure B will be short on detail, of course. In discussing contrasts between their written responses and Visual 13.1, emphasize the point that Visual 13.1 shows America's forests to be, according to some measures, abundant and productive.

D. Some students may be surprised to learn that conditions in the nation's forests look favorable — by any measure. Build on that response (or, if necessary, introduce the point yourself): The good news about our forests might well seem surprising. After all, media reports often focus on news of environmental degradation. Nonetheless, we have enabled our forests to expand. We must value forests highly. But why? What is it about forests that might explain our interest in them and our support for their growth?

LESSON 13

Possible responses: forests are a source of timber — an important resource; forests provide for wildlife and plant habitat, fostering biodiversity; forests provide an attractive environment for hikers, campers and cross-country skiers; forests contribute to improved water and air quality.

E. Against this background of reasons for our interest in abundant, healthy forests, introduce a troublesome fact: Our national forests, especially those in the Western states, have been severely damaged in recent years by wildfires. **Display Visual 13.2.** Call on volunteers to read the Visual. Discuss main points briefly. Underscore the point that most large fires occur in the Western states, where most forest land is federally owned.

F. **Display Visual 13.3** and state the mystery that is central to this lesson: Americans value forests for many reasons. Nobody wants to see wildfires devastate forests. But devastation from fire is a real threat for many forests today, especially our national forests in the West. How has the threat of catastrophic fires come about?

Possible responses: a recent history of bad drought conditions, especially in the West; lightning strikes; more people living near forest areas; human carelessness; arson.

G. In discussing the students' responses, explain that drought, lightning strikes, and human carelessness all help to explain how wildfires get started. But how fires get started is not the only thing that needs to be explained. After all, lightning strikes always have been around to set fires off, especially in dry weather. But the fires set off in this way have not always turned out to be intense, huge, and destructive, on the order of many recent fires.

H. If wildfires today tend to be more destructive than the small, frequent fires that have been common in the past, what might explain the change? Tell the students that they will consider this question by reference to Activity 13.1.

I. **Distribute a copy of Activity 13.1** to each student. Divide the class into groups of three or four. Assign the students to read the Activity, discuss the questions posed, and respond to each question. When the groups finish their work, call on students from each group to summarize their responses to the questions.

Answers:

1. *In the old ponderosa pine forests, frequent, naturally occurring fires kept the underbrush burned down. As a result, the forests were uncluttered and dotted with open, grassy areas that provided wildlife habitat. Today, forests in the West are typically cluttered with dense undergrowth, so that trees must struggle for moisture and nourishment. The grassy meadows have largely disappeared.*

2. *Possible responses: Today's forests do not get thinned. Fires are suppressed as quickly as possible, and few trees are cut on publicly owned land.*

3. *Forests today are more vulnerable to intense, catastrophic fires because the buildup of brush on forest floors creates fuel for fires, and the fires that do ignite spread quickly from tree to tree in the dense, crowded conditions.*

J. **Display Visual 13.4.** Ask:

How might a long history of fire-suppression efforts by the Forest Service be related to the condition of forest density and fuel buildup described in Activity 13.1?

It would change the composition of the forests, fostering density and increasing the fuel load in the forest understory.

K. How might a decrease in timber harvesting be related to the condition of forest density and fuel buildup described in Activity 13.1?

Timber harvesting is a forest-management practice that reduces forest density and the buildup of fuel loads. As timber harvesting decreases, density and fuel buildups increase.

L. If you wanted to create vast tinderboxes — dense forests stoked with fuel likely to burn hot and fast — how might you go about the task?

Try to extinguish all fires in the forests as quickly as possible, no matter where or how small they might be. Also, reduce timber cutting in the forests nearly to zero. Taken together, these two policies would do much to produce the tinderbox effect.

M. In concluding the discussion of Visual 13.4, emphasize the point that nobody accuses the Forest Service of having created forest tinderboxes intentionally. In settling on a policy of fire suppression and in overseeing a steep downturn in timber cutting, Forest Service officials probably did what all of us do as we make decisions. They probably responded to incentives.

N. Write the word *Incentive* on the board. Remind the students of EcoDetection principle 4. Explain that an incentive is something that encourages people to act — to make a certain decision or to take a certain action. Parents who reward their children for getting good grades, for example, create an incentive for their children to study hard. When we want to explain why people behave as they do, it usually helps to look at the incentives that might be influencing them.

O. In the case of the Forest Service helping to create tinderbox forests, what might the incentives have been? **Distribute copies of Activity 13.2.** Divide the class into groups of three or four. Assign the students to read the Activity, discuss the questions posed, and respond in writing to each question. When the groups finish their work, call on students from each group to summarize their responses. Discuss their responses and note common themes, focusing on claims students make about the incentives at stake and how those incentives might influence policy decisions.

Possible responses: The money flow and the regulatory climate create incentives for the Forest Service to make fire suppression a top priority.

P. Extend the discussion of responses to Activity 13.2 by posing this question: Could things be different? Or, to put it differently, what would it take to bring about a shift in priorities, so that forest-management efforts could be redirected toward goals of forest restoration? Explain that we can glimpse some of the possibilities by looking at examples of forests outside the national forest system where programs of active management have opened forests up — reducing the risk of catastrophic fire while also enhancing forest health and environmental quality.

Q. **Distribute copies of Activity 13.3.** Divide the class into groups of three or four. Assign the students to read the Activity, discuss the questions posed, and respond in writing to each question. When the groups have finished their work, call on students to summarize their responses. Discuss their responses and take note of main themes, especially regarding the incentives created by private ownership of forest land in the International Paper Company case.

Possible responses: Private ownership of the forests enabled International Paper to engage in timber cutting. IP wanted to cut timber in order to earn profits. The profit motive also created an incentive to maintain the health of the forests for use by campers, hunters and hikers.

R. Summarize the main points of the lesson:

- The threat of wildfire in our national forests is heightened by tinderbox conditions.

- Tinderbox conditions are created by forest density and the buildup of fuel loads in the forest understory.

- Forest density and fuel buildup have been unintended consequences of forest-management and environmental policy — products of decades of fire suppression and constraints on timber cutting.

- The emphasis on fire suppression rather than fire prevention can be explained in part as a response to incentives. The Forest Service is doing what it might be expected to do, given the funding system and the environmental regulations with which it works.

- To change conditions in the national forests, it would be necessary to change the incentives that shape the decisions of forest managers. Possibilities of that sort can be inferred from cases in which private owners of forest land manage forests well in order to protect the forests' commercial value.

LESSON 13

ASSESSMENT

Multiple-Choice Questions

1. Most large wildfires occur in forests
   - a. near crowded urban areas.
   - b. in Georgia.
   - c. on the east coast.
   - **d. in the West.**

2. Most forests in the West are
   - **a. federally owned.**
   - b. state owned.
   - c. county owned.
   - d. privately owned.

3. In its approach to the problem of wildfires, the U.S. Forest Service has strongly emphasized
   - a. a policy of fire prevention.
   - **b. a policy of fire suppression.**
   - c. a policy of "let 'em burn."
   - d. a policy of cloud seeding to increase rainfalls.

4. Timber harvesting in America's national forests
   - a. has increased steadily since 1910.
   - b. has left most national forests stripped bare of trees.
   - c. has provided much-needed tax revenue for school districts in the Western states.
   - **d. has decreased a great deal since the 1980s.**

Essay Questions

1. You are discussing the problem of wildfires with a friend. "I don't see what is so complicated about it," your friend says. "People are careless with matches and campfires, and we have had a lot of dry weather recently in the West. That's why we've had so many bad fires." What is your friend overlooking in these remarks?

Carelessness and drought help to explain how fires get started. They don't explain why many fires recently have become huge problems — burning intensively and spreading uncontrollably to devastate large areas. Fires of that sort develop because the forests have become tinderboxes — overgrown and cluttered with dead wood and brush that have accumulated for years. The buildup of fuel loads has been an unintended consequence of policies intended to protect the forests — fire suppression policies and policies that restrict timber cutting.

2. Suppose that you owned two million acres of forest land. And suppose that you have scheduled a meeting with two consultants to get advice about how to manage your forests.

   - **Consultant A says,** "Put out every fire as soon as one pops up. Other than that, don't touch the land. Don't cut a single tree. Then you can preserve your forests in all their natural beauty."

   - **Consultant B says,** "Keep your forests thinned out so that big, fire-resistant trees can flourish. Then you won't have to worry so much about fires. You'll also provide better wildlife habitat."

Which line of advice would you follow? Why? Explain your answer

Answers should reflect an understanding of the consequences likely to follow from each line of advice. The advice given by Consultant A would result in a dense, cluttered forest with underbrush collecting on the forest floor. Over time, the underbrush would create tinderbox conditions, ideal for igniting fires. Those fires would be likely to burn intensely and spread rapidly from tree to tree. The advice given by Consultant B would result in a less crowded forest, with larger trees and less undergrowth. In such a forest, fires would be less likely to ignite and less likely to burn out of control if they did ignite.

VISUAL 13.1

ARE OUR FORESTS DISAPPEARING?

- Between 1970 and 1990, the number of wooded acres in the United States grew by 20 percent.

- In 1990, average annual wood growth in the United States was three times higher than in 1920.

- In Vermont, between 1893 and 1993, land areas covered by forest increased from 35 percent to 76 percent.

- In the four states of Maine, New Hampshire, Vermont and New York, forest areas increased by 26 million acres between 1900 and 1993.

- Increasingly abundant forests in the United States have supported population growth among certain wildlife species once rarely seen, including timber wolves and bald eagles.

- Abundant forests also support an important industry. As of 2002, the United States was a major producer of commercial wood, accounting for one quarter of the world's total output.

Sources:
1. H. Salwasser, "Gaining Perspective," Journal of Forestry (November 1990).
2. R. Sedjo, "The Fires This Time: Indecision at the Forest Service,"
   PERC Reports (June 2002).

VISUAL 13.2

WILDFIRES: A FACT SHEET

- On average, wildfires consume more than four million acres of forests per year in the United States.

- In 2000, 7.5 million acres of forests burned. This is an area roughly equal to the size of Massachusetts, Rhode Island and Delaware combined.

- In 2001, 84,079 separate fires burned about 3.5 million acres of forests.

- In 2002, 88,458 separate fires burned 6.9 million acres of forests.

- Most large wildfires occur in the Western states. Four of the largest 10 fires in 2000 occurred in Idaho, while two were in Alaska. The others were in Wyoming, Montana, Washington, and Oregon.

- More than 60 percent of all Western forests are federally owned.

- About 70 percent of all forests in the Eastern states are privately owned.

- The U.S. Forest Service estimates that 190 million acres of federal forests and rangeland — an area twice the size of California — now face a high, ongoing risk of catastrophic fire.

Sources:
1. Cambridge Scientific Abstracts, "Environmental Hot Topics: Wildfires, Fuel Loads, and Forest Management Policy Issues" (January 2004).
2. U.S. Forest Service fact sheets.
3. University of Washington, "Without Thinning the Worst Is Yet to Come for Fire-prone Forests." See http://www.washington.edu/newsroom/news/2003archive/09-03archive/k092603.html.

VISUAL 13.3

THE MYSTERY OF THE FIRES THAT NOBODY WANTS

Nobody wants to see wildfires devastate forests. But devastation from fire is a threat for many forests today, especially our national forests in the West. How has the threat of catastrophic fires come about?

VISUAL 13.4

HOW DID OUR FORESTS BECOME TINDERBOXES?

- In the summer of 1910, a fire exploded in the Bitterroot Mountains and raged across Montana, Idaho and Washington, burning about three million acres of forests. Smoke darkened the skies far to the east, giving city dwellers a glimpse of the fires at a distance. News about the fires traumatized the public and prompted Congress to pass legislation that would, for the first time, provide federal money to be spent on fighting forest fires. The initial goal was to put out every reported fire by 10 a.m. the next day.

- By 1926, the U.S. Forest Service had developed a policy of fire suppression. It sought to extinguish all wildfires in forests before they reached 10 acres in size. Fire suppression served as a top priority for the Forest Service at least until the 1970s. It remains an important priority today.

- Today, very little timber is harvested from federally owned forests. Timber harvests from national forests have fallen by about 85 percent since the 1980s. The United States is a major supplier of commercial wood, but less than five percent of the output comes from federally owned forests.

Sources:
1. *Cambridge Scientific Abstracts, "Environmental Hot Topics: Wildfires, Fuel Loads, and Forest Management Policy Issues" (January 2004).*
2. *L. Platts, "Politics Manages Our Public Lands," PERC Reports (September 2002).*
3. *R. Sedjo, "The Fires This Time: Indecision at the Forest Service," PERC Reports (June 2002).*

ACTIVITY 13.1

THAT WAS THEN, THIS IS NOW

Name_____

What were America's forests like 150 years ago? How have they changed since then? Information from old photographs, pioneers' journals and other sources provide a basis for comparison.

Read the two accounts below. Discuss the Questions for Discussion with other members of your group. Then respond in writing to those questions.

THAT WAS THEN

A hundred and fifty years ago, ponderosa pine covered nearly 40 million acres of the American West. Fires occurring as often as every 7 to 25 years burned the forest understory (the layer of vegetation beneath the main forest canopy) while leaving hardy, fire-resistant pine unharmed. As a result, forests were uncluttered. Before Europeans arrived, there were typically 30 to 60 large trees per acre in the area that is now the Okanogan National Forest in Washington. Early settlers could drive their wagons through park-like savannas under towering trees, pausing to rest in the open meadows that dotted the forest landscape. In a journal entry she wrote in 1853, for example, Rebecca Ketcham reported that "our road has been nearly the whole day through the woods, that is, if beautiful groves of pine trees can be called woods…The country all through is burnt over, so often there is not the least underbrush, but the grass grows thick and beautiful." Besides providing pleasant passageways and views for travelers, these grassy, open areas also provided willows, berries and other food sources for wildlife.

THIS IS NOW

Today's forests in the West are quite different. In many of them, an understory of shade-tolerant Douglas fir has grown so dense that it is difficult for people or animals to squeeze through the thickets. In the Okanogan National Forest, for example, the average today is 1,000 trees per acre, and in some places the number is as high as 3,000. In such circumstances, trees compete for moisture and nourishment, leaving them in poor health and vulnerable to insects and disease. The grassy meadows and small, sunny openings have largely disappeared, along with the forage they once provided for wildlife.

Questions for Discussion

1. According to these two descriptions, what major changes have occurred in the forests of the West over the past 150 years?

2. The two descriptions do not explain what caused the changes to occur. What might some of the causes be?

3. Which forests would be more vulnerable to intense, catastrophic fires—the forests then or now? Why?

Sources:

1. H.L. Fretwell, Public Lands Forests: Do We Get What We Pay For? PERC, July 1999.

2. University of Washington, "Without Thinning the Worst Is Yet to Come for Fire-prone Forests."
    See http://www.washington.edu/newsroom/news/2003archive/k092603.html.

ACTIVITY 13.2

WHAT WOULD YOU DO IF YOU RAN THE FORESTS?

Name_____

Imagine that you are a senior official in the U.S. Forest Service, serving on a task force responsible for developing forest-management policies. In particular, you must tackle the problem of wildfires. Together with other members of the task force, you have identified two broad approaches to the problem:

- *The fire-suppression approach.* Big fires produce nasty results. They destroy a valuable resource. They destroy wildlife habitat. They spew carbon dioxide into the air. They cause soil erosion and degrade waterways. And they often pose a threat to human life, especially when they get out of hand. It makes sense, therefore, to try to put fires out as quickly as possible — all of them. After all, big fires start out as little fires.

- *The fire-prevention approach.* The problem isn't fires, exactly. The problem is huge, intense, catastrophic fires. The goal of forest management should be to prevent fires of that sort. Prevention efforts should emphasize active forest management, aimed at restoring healthy, open, fire-resistant forests. Management of this sort would make use of forest thinning, prescribed burns and timber sales. These practices would reduce the fuel loads that now create tinderbox conditions in many of our national forests. They also would improve wildlife habitat in the forests and enhance scenic beauty.

You want to select the best approach, of course. In thinking about what that might be, the following two points keep popping up in your mind.

- *The money flow.* It costs somewhere between $400 and $500 per acre to fight forest fires. The costs include salary money paid every summer to men and women who find seasonal employment fighting fires. The U.S. Congress provides the Forest Service with a blank check to cover these firefighting costs. The bills are paid with tax dollars from emergency funds, not from the Forest Service budget. In contrast, the Forest Service must pay for fire-prevention projects (including forest thinning and controlled burns) out of its annually appropriated budget. As of 1999, Congress allotted the Forest Service $1.25 per acre for fire-prevention services. Effective fire-prevention requires, most experts believe, expenditures of $40 to $50 per acre, at minimum.

- *The regulatory climate.* Since about 1970, Congress and the federal regulatory agencies have put into effect more than 200 new laws and regulations bearing on the management of national forests. These laws and regulations are intended to protect the environment. Some of them establish procedures by means of which citizens can object to various forest-management decisions — regarding timber cutting, thinning or controlled burning in areas known to provide habitat for endangered species, for example. When objections are made, the public hearings and appeals that follow can stretch out over years, obliging the Forest Service to spend a great deal of time and money on the task of explaining and defending its proposed actions.

ACTIVITY 13.2, CONTINUED

Questions for Discussion

1. As a Forest Service official, you know that the Forest Service will get paid with a blank check for firefighting services, and you know that the Service will have to pay out of its regular budget for fire-prevention services. What incentives are created by this money flow?

2. You also know that proposals for thinning or timber cutting in the national forests are apt to be met by objections based on environmental concerns, and you know that responding to these objections will require Forest Service officials and lawyers to be engaged in lengthy, expensive deliberations. What incentives are created by the regulatory climate you face?

3. Taking account of the incentives you have identified in response to questions 1 and 2, are you more likely to favor a high priority for fire suppression or fire prevention in Forest Service policies and practices?

LESSON 13

ACTIVITY 13.3

PRIVATE OWNERSHIP, PROFITS AND ENVIRONMENTAL QUALITY

Name_____

Many residents of Arkansas, Louisiana and Texas enjoy camping, hunting and year-round outdoor activity. Without free access to large areas of public lands such as those in the West, these outdoor enthusiasts often look elsewhere for pine forests, wooded streams and other attractive environments. In the past, some relied on the International Paper Company (IP) to provide them with free use of its 1.2 million acres of private timberlands. While permitting recreational uses of its property, the company still managed its forests with one goal in mind: Timber production, the main source of its revenue.

By the early 1980s, however, steadily increasing demand for recreation convinced IP executives that it would make sense to begin charging fees for recreation. Through the sale of daily-use permits, seasonal family permits and multi-year leases to hunting clubs, the company generated significant revenue. From no revenue in 1980, recreation-related revenue grew to $2 million in 1986, accounting for 25 percent of the company's profits in the region. By 1999, IP earnings from non-timber sources reached $5 million. As profits grew, so did the incentive to manage the forests for recreation as well as timber.

To enhance wildlife production, IP maintained corridors of trees between timber-harvest areas for wildlife movement. In areas that would previously have been clear-cut, IP left clumps of trees standing to provide greater age diversity. IP reduced the overall size of timber cuts; it made the perimeters of cut-over areas irregular to attract a greater variety of wildlife. It restricted timber cutting along the banks of streams. It entered into long-term contracts with hunting clubs, thus providing club members with an incentive to take good care of the land they leased.

These efforts have paid big dividends — to wildlife populations in the area and to company shareholders. Game surveys in 1996 showed that populations of whitetail deer had increased fivefold and turkey populations tenfold. There were also substantial increases in fox, quail, ducks and non-game populations.

The incentive for IP to change its land management priorities came from the revenues generated by fee-based recreation programs and the growing interest in sustainable forest management.

Source: H. L. Fretwell, Public Lands Forests: Do We Get What We Pay For? PERC (July 1999), p. 18.

Questions for Discussion

1. Imagine a different starting point. What if the IP forests in the early 1980s had been very similar in their composition to the national forests of the West — densely covered over with small trees and brush, and offering no open areas? How would that have affected people's interest in using the land for outdoor recreation?

2. In the national forests, very little timber cutting is done. But IP continued to cut timber even after it stepped up its offerings of recreational opportunities. What made it possible for IP to continue cutting timber?

3. By harvesting timber, IP made a lot of money. Why didn't it harvest all its timber so that it could make even more money?

4. In this case, what was the relationship between private ownership of forest land and environmental quality?

How Could We Cut Back on the Garbage We Produce?

LESSON 14

HOW COULD WE CUT BACK ON THE GARBAGE WE PRODUCE?

LESSON DESCRIPTION

Students discuss the concept of *price* and investigate how prices can influence people's decisions to buy groceries and generate garbage, depending on what sort of price system is used. Then students apply what they know about prices in an effort to solve a garbage-collection mystery.

BACKGROUND

Disposing of household solid waste (garbage, trash) raises sensitive environmental issues in most communities. As communities grow, garbage piles up quickly in landfills, and building new, safe landfills is sometimes expensive. Many cities have tried with mixed success to reduce the total amount of garbage they must deal with by asking citizens to create less of it — by reusing things, recycling things or buying fewer things in the first place. Reducing the total amount of garbage would extend the life of current landfills and lessen the need to build new ones.

ECOMYSTERY

The Philadelphia suburb of Perkasie grew in population throughout the 1980s. Despite its growth, Perkasie succeeded in reducing the amount of garbage collected from its residents. It also reduced its garbage-collection costs by 40 percent. Neighboring communities, meanwhile, collected garbage in increasing amounts and faced increasing garbage-collection costs. How did Perkasie do it?

ECONOMIC REASONING

The garbage problem is directly related to the price paid for garbage-collection services. It is also related to the system of pricing used. To see why, think about the incentives that pricing systems can create. Homeowners typically pay a flat fee, once a year, for garbage-collection services, regardless of the volume of garbage they load into their trash cans. Increasing the flat fee rarely changes the amount of garbage people set out to be collected. But increasing flat fees is not the only option available to communities. They also can make use of per-bag fees for garbage collection (EcoDetection prin-

ciple 5). Per-bag pricing creates an incentive to conserve on garbage production (EcoDetection principles 2 and 4). When homeowners must pay per-bag for the garbage they produce, they tend to produce less of it, and the total volume of garbage sent to the landfill decreases accordingly (EcoDetection principle 3).

ECONOMIC CONCEPTS

- Choice
- Cost
- Incentives
- Price

OBJECTIVES

Students will:

1. Explain how different methods of pricing will cause consumers to change their behavior.

2. Use principles of EcoDetection to select useful clues and solve a garbage mystery.

3. Explain why increasing flat fees for garbage service will not reduce the amount of garbage created by an average household.

CONTENT STANDARDS

- People respond predictably to positive and negative incentives. (NCEE Content Standard 4.)

- Prices send signals and provide incentives to buyers and sellers. When supply or demand changes, market prices adjust, affecting incentives. (NCEE Content Standard 8.)

TIME

45 minutes

MATERIALS

- A transparency of Visual 14.1 and a copy of Visual 14.1 (see Procedure H, below) for each student

- A copy of Activity 14.1, duplicated and cut apart so that each student can receive two or three clues (see Procedure H, below)

- Optional source for teachers: T. Tregarthen and S. Tregarthen, "Garbage by the Bag: Perkasie Acts on Solid Waste." *The Margin* (Sept./Oct. 1989), 17.

PROCEDURE

A. Explain to the students that in this lesson they are going to make a comparison between grocery shopping and garbage collection. Then they are going to solve an environmental mystery using economic reasoning.

B. Show them a copy of a grocery store advertisement displaying many items and their prices.

C. Ask the students to jot down notes on what they would buy from the store if they had $30 to spend on groceries. Anything goes: they may buy chips and soda or brown rice and vegetables. Call on some students to tell about their choices; put a few examples on the board for everyone to see.

D. Next ask the students what they would buy if they were told that — for a flat fee of $30 a month — they could go to the grocery store and buy whatever they wanted, and as much of it as they wanted.

Given this alternative, they probably would elect to buy more and better food, and to buy more often.

E. Ask the students to explain the change in what they say they would buy. We are imagining that it is the same store, the same food, and the same $30, yet in the second case the students have said they would behave very differently as consumers.

The incentives have changed. With per-item pricing, the shopper must keep the total purchase within the $30 limit. With the flat-fee arrangement, the total amount of items purchased does not increase the total amount of money spent. Flat fees do not encourage people to conserve on their purchases.

F. Introduce the next activity. Explain that it will extend the line of thought illustrated in the grocery-shopping example. Keeping that example in mind, the students will try to solve a mystery about garbage collection.

G. **Display Visual 14.1** and discuss the mystery briefly. Remind the students to approach the mystery by means of economic reasoning. A good starting point is the principle that people are influenced by incentives.

H. Divide the class into groups of three or four students. **Hand each student two or three clues, produced from Activity 14.1.** Be sure that each group has all nine of the clues listed on Activity 14.1. **Give each group a copy of the mystery in**

Visual 14.1. Then ask the groups to solve the mystery on Visual 14.1, using the principles of EcoDetection. Provide these directions:

1. The students have two tasks: First, to decide which clues are useful for solving the mystery; second, to write out a solution to the mystery and record it on the chalkboard.

2. The students do not need to spend time arguing about whether a given clue is true or false. All the clues are true. But some clues are relevant to solving the mystery and some are not.

3. Each group should elect a leader to lead the small-group discussion and report its results.

4. Each student has at least two clues. It is each student's responsibility to read that clue to the rest of the group and determine its value in solving the mystery.

I. Monitor the group discussions. You may find that students are eager to have their clues thought of as important. Some may go to extremes of tortured logic to argue that their clues are crucial. Remind the students as necessary that this exercise involves sorting out the useful clues from the irrelevant ones, and that they can use the principles of EcoDetection for help in making those choices.

J. Ask each group to report and explain its solution to the mystery.

Suggested answer: Many garbage-collection systems charge a flat fee for garbage service. This price system does not reward people for reducing trash quantities, nor does it penalize them for increasing the amount of their garbage. So raising a flat fee as suggested in clue 6 will not encourage people to minimize their garbage. Clue 5 makes it clear that the leaders of Perkasie decided to present their citizens with a different price system, a per-bag fee, which rewarded those who conserved and penalized those who increased their garbage. While most citizens favored the convenience of city garbage pick-up, a fee for each bag provided an incentive for people to use the minimum number of bags (and to pack them very full). Of course, individuals still had the alternative of using more bags if they needed to. However, clues 3 and 9 make it clear that most Perkasians decided to conserve on their use of bags, thus reducing the amount of trash to be collected as well as the costs of collection. Clues 1, 2, 6, 7 and 8 provide interesting

Lesson 14

background for the story, but they are not useful in explaining the mystery.

K. Note to the teacher: One downside of per-bag fee systems is that they may encourage illegal dumping of garbage. Some people don't want to pay a fee each time they have garbage to dispose of, so they may risk dumping it illegally to avoid the costs. Some communities have addressed this problem by instituting a flat-fee charge for a certain amount of garbage and then charging per-bag fees after the base level has been exceeded.

CLOSURE

Ask the students to review the main points of the lesson.

1. How does a per-item price system influence the amount of garbage people produce and the amount of groceries they buy?

    A per-item price system encourages people to consider the costs and benefits of each additional item — purchased or set out as trash — and to conserve on the total amount purchased or set out as trash.

2. How does a flat-fee price system influence the amount of garbage people produce and the amount of groceries they buy?

    A flat-fee price is essentially the cost of the first purchase. After it is paid, all other items are free because the price will not change. Therefore, flat-fee pricing encourages the purchase of many more grocery items and much more garbage. By buying many things and putting out a lot of trash, people feel they are "getting their money's worth."

3. Will increasing a flat fee cause people to consume fewer groceries and produce less garbage?

    No. The increase probably will encourage them to consume even more groceries and produce more garbage so that they "get their money's worth."

ASSESSMENT

Multiple-Choice Questions

1. Per-bag fees for garbage disposal influence people in which of the following ways:

    a. They reduce the cost of garbage disposal for people who minimize their output of garbage.

    b. They increase the cost of garbage disposal for people who minimize their output of garbage.

    c. They double the cost of garbage disposal for people who minimize their output of garbage.

    d. They reduce the cost of garbage disposal for people who increase their output of garbage.

2. Which of the following price systems encourages consumers to minimize the amounts they purchase?

    a. A higher per-item price

    b. A lower per-item price

    c. A higher flat-fee price

    d. A lower flat-fee price

Essay Questions

1. What difference does it make whether residents are charged a flat fee for garbage disposal or a per-bag fee? In either case, the fee is just a message to residents about how much garbage disposal costs in that community. Respond.

    Consumers will tend to conserve on their garbage disposal under a per-bag price system, to minimize their personal costs. Under a flat-fee system, their personal costs are the same whether they conserve on producing garbage or not, so they will tend not to conserve.

2. Respond to this statement made by a city council member in charge of the garbage disposal system:

    "In college I took an economics course and learned how prices influence people's behavior. If you raise prices, people will purchase less of a service like garbage collection. So I think the city should raise its yearly assessment for garbage service from $100 to $2,000. A $2,000 cost to the city's residents would make them think twice about disposing of unnecessary garbage."

    The city council member only learned part of the story. If the city's residents pay an annual flat fee, they only pay once for their garbage service. With this system, they pay, essentially, for the first pickup. There are no new charges after that, so every pickup after the first one is free. Under such a system, therefore, residents will toss out anything remotely resembling garbage in order to "get their money's worth." If it were implemented, this council member's plan would encourage people to dispose of greater volumes of garbage.

VISUAL 14.1

THE MYSTERY OF THE DISAPPEARING GARBAGE

The Philadelphia suburb of Perkasie grew in population throughout the 1980s. Despite its growth, however, Perkasie succeeded in reducing the amount of garbage it collected from its residents. It also succeeded in reducing its garbage-collection costs by 40 percent. Neighboring communities, meanwhile, collected garbage in increasing amounts and faced increased garbage-collection costs. How did Perkasie do it?

Lesson 14

Activity 14.1

Clues

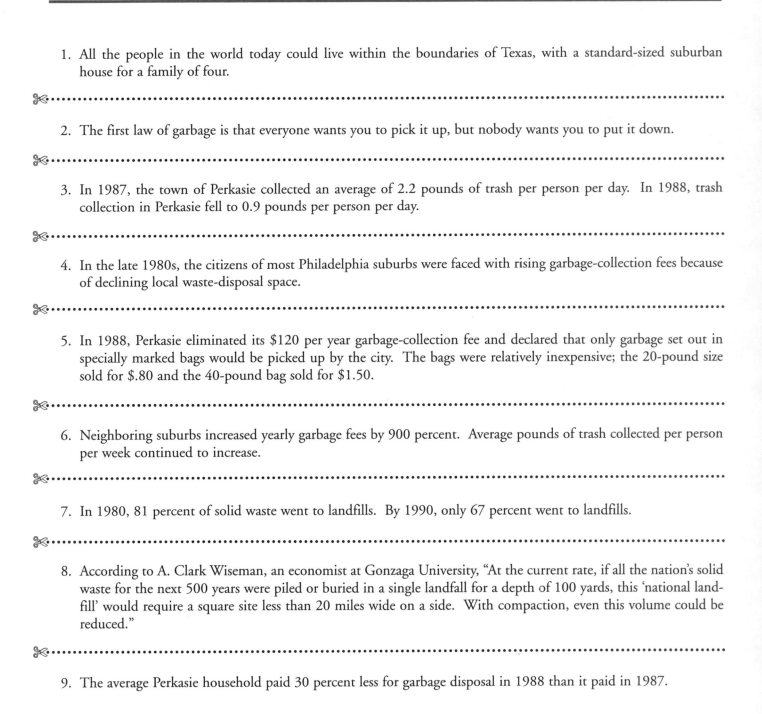

1. All the people in the world today could live within the boundaries of Texas, with a standard-sized suburban house for a family of four.

....

2. The first law of garbage is that everyone wants you to pick it up, but nobody wants you to put it down.

....

3. In 1987, the town of Perkasie collected an average of 2.2 pounds of trash per person per day. In 1988, trash collection in Perkasie fell to 0.9 pounds per person per day.

....

4. In the late 1980s, the citizens of most Philadelphia suburbs were faced with rising garbage-collection fees because of declining local waste-disposal space.

....

5. In 1988, Perkasie eliminated its $120 per year garbage-collection fee and declared that only garbage set out in specially marked bags would be picked up by the city. The bags were relatively inexpensive; the 20-pound size sold for $.80 and the 40-pound bag sold for $1.50.

....

6. Neighboring suburbs increased yearly garbage fees by 900 percent. Average pounds of trash collected per person per week continued to increase.

....

7. In 1980, 81 percent of solid waste went to landfills. By 1990, only 67 percent went to landfills.

....

8. According to A. Clark Wiseman, an economist at Gonzaga University, "At the current rate, if all the nation's solid waste for the next 500 years were piled or buried in a single landfall for a depth of 100 yards, this 'national land-fill' would require a square site less than 20 miles wide on a side. With compaction, even this volume could be reduced."

....

9. The average Perkasie household paid 30 percent less for garbage disposal in 1988 than it paid in 1987.

HOW PRIVATE EFFORTS CAN IMPROVE ENVIRONMENTAL QUALITY

Lesson 15

How Private Efforts Can Improve Environmental Quality

Lesson Description

The students examine case studies showing how various uses of private property affect environmental quality. They analyze these cases in order to identify conditions under which private property ownership and the profit motive create incentives for environmental protection.

Background

When people talk about environmental issues, they often make strong assumptions about markets, profits and government regulation. It is the search for profits or private advantages — according to these assumptions — that pushes people to act without regard for harmful effects on the environment. Environmental protection, therefore, is said to involve a difficult struggle against markets and the search for profits. This struggle is said to pit those who seek to protect their own advantages, on the one side, against those on the other side who seek to defend, through government regulations, a larger, public interest in environmental quality.

Environmental policy in the United States has been influenced strongly by these assumptions over the past 30 years. Laws and regulations governing water, air, public land and endangered species have multiplied. Some of the regulations have produced important environmental improvements. The bald eagle population in the United States has benefited, for example, from regulations banning the use of DDT.

But the regulatory approach has not always succeeded. Some regulations have produced small benefits at high costs. Others have produced unwelcome, unintended results — creating incentives for private landowners to harvest timber stands prematurely, for example, before an anticipated restriction on timber cutting can take effect. And in those parts of the world where markets, private property and the profit motive were prohibited by governmental fiat throughout much of the twentieth century, the environment, we know now, has been seriously degraded.

Observations of this sort have prompted many people to rethink popular assumptions about environmental protection in favor of an alternative view. The alternative view is that market forces and institutions — including private property and the incentives created by a profit system — have an important role to play in efforts to improve environmental quality.

EcoMystery

Many examples suggest that people seeking profits or their own private advantage have harmed the environment. Since this is so, why shouldn't environmental protection be set aside as a special goal to be sought through government regulation? How could private property and profits play any positive role in protecting the environment?

Economic Reasoning

Owners of private property make decisions about how to use their property, weighing anticipated costs and benefits (EcoDetection principles 1 and 2). If they face pressure to use their property in a way that will impose costs on them, they may resist, even when the issue at stake involves environmental quality. Resistance is less likely when environmental quality is pursued as something to be produced through voluntary exchanges between the people who demand it and the people in a position to supply it. Because many people are willing to pay for experiences associated with environmental quality, owners of private property sometimes can earn profits by supplying such experiences to anglers, hunters, hikers, bird-watchers and others. In these cases, the profit motive encourages property owners to protect the environment (EcoDetection principles 3 and 4).

Economic Concepts

- Benefits
- Costs
- Incentives
- Private property
- Profits
- Voluntary exchange

LESSON 15

OBJECTIVES

Students will:

1. Analyze environmental issues by reference to costs, benefits and incentives.

2. Explain how actions undertaken for profit can also improve the environment.

CONTENT STANDARDS

- Different methods can be used to allocate goods and services. People, acting individually or collectively through government, must choose which methods to use to allocate different kinds of goods and services. (NCEE Content Standard 3.)

- People respond predictably to positive and negative incentives. (NCEE Content Standard 4.)

- Voluntary exchange occurs only when all participating parties expect to gain. This is true for trade among individuals or organizations within a nation, and among individuals or organizations in different nations. (NCEE Content Standard 5.)

- Markets exist when buyers and sellers interact. This interaction determines market prices and thereby allocates scarce goods and services. (NCEE Content Standard 7.)

- Institutions evolve in market economies to help individuals and groups accomplish their goals. Banks, labor unions, corporations, legal systems, and not-for-profit organizations are examples of important institutions. A different kind of institution, clearly defined and well enforced property rights, is essential to a market economy. (NCEE Content Standard 10.)

- Entrepreneurs are people who take the risk of organizing productive resources to make goods and services. Profit is an important incentive that leads entrepreneurs to accept the risks of business failure. (NCEE Content Standard 14.)

TIME

75 minutes

MATERIALS

- A transparency of Visuals 15.1 and 15.2
- A copy of Activities 15.1, 15.2 and 15.3 for each student

PROCEDURE

A. Tell the students that in this lesson they will study examples of how individual decisions about environmental problems are influenced by property rights and considerations of costs and benefits.

B. Explain that environmental problems often seem to be caused by people seeking to reduce their costs and increase their profits. To provide an example, **display Visual 15.1.** Ask:

1. Why didn't the taconite companies haul all the waste material they generated off to a secure waste-disposal site instead of dumping it into the lake?

   Students may suggest that, at the time, nobody knew the waste was harmful; also, there may have been no secure waste-disposal sites; and anyway, hauling the waste away would have been expensive. It probably was a lot cheaper for the mining companies to dump it into the lake.

2. If dumping the waste into the lake helped the taconite companies cut their costs, how would that have affected their profits?

   Profit is the money you have left over after paying off your costs. If you can reduce your costs, you probably can increase your profits.

C. Explain that the taconite case seems to provide a clear example of how seeking profit can cause businesses to ignore the environmental effects of their actions — especially when there are no regulations in effect to restrain them. But there is another important element in the taconite case. To see what that element is, the students should consider this question: What if the taconite companies had trucked all their waste materials down the shore of Lake Superior to the city of Duluth and dumped the stuff on people's lawns? What would have happened?

   The owners of the homes would have called the police, charging criminal trespass; then they would have sued the mining companies. You can't just dump stuff on people's property. Because it is theirs, the owners get to decide whether their property can be used as a dump or not.

LESSON 15

D. Why didn't the same thing happen when mining companies dumped waste into Lake Superior?

The lake didn't seem to be owned by anybody. No private owners could come forward to object to the dumping.

E. Underscore the importance of the private-law-suits-that-didn't-happen in the taconite case: When ownership of property is clearly established and protected within a system of laws, people seeking profits can't easily abuse that property. If they do, they'll get hit with lawsuits and perhaps criminal trespass charges.

F. Moving along from the taconite case, ask the students to consider a different example, one involving Luke Seedy. Seedy owns a piece of property in a remote area. His property is not well suited for farming or residential development, but Luke uses it once or twice a year as a site for auctions he conducts for local residents. He also raises bees on the property and pastures a few goats. One Friday night at the Crossroads Tap, Seedy meets Friendly Jack Salvage — a guy who scrounges up old cars and sells them for parts and scrap metal. Jack is looking for a place to store a few hundred wrecked cars he has collected from around the state, and he offers to rent Seedy's property as a storage yard for the cars for $500 per month. Ask:

1. Could Friendly Jack just come in at night and dump his cars on Seedy's property?

   No.

2. What other alternative does Friendly Jack have?

   He can, as noted, make Seedy an offer: "In return for the use of your property as a storage yard for my wrecked cars, I will pay you $500 per month" — or whatever Friendly Jack thinks he could afford to pay and Seedy might be willing to accept.

3. In considering Friendly Jack's offer, what might Seedy think about in deciding whether to accept it or not?

   Does he want to let somebody use his property at all, or would he prefer to retain it in its present condition for his own use? If he would like to make it available for somebody else's use, is Jack's offer the best one he could get? Or could he get a deal more to his liking by renting his property out to somebody else for a different purpose?

G. In concluding the discussion of Friendly Jack and his offer, underscore the point that when people make decisions about how to use property they own, they weigh the costs and benefits of the different alternatives available to them. They might be willing to allow others to use their property — giving up their own use of it to make that possible. But if they do agree to such an arrangement, they would ordinarily expect to be compensated for what they give up in the exchange.

H. Tell the students that they will turn next to an example in which property rights have a bearing on a well-known environmental issue. **Distribute a copy of Activity 15.1** to each student. Divide the class into groups of two or three. Assign the groups to read the Activity, discuss the questions posed, and respond to those questions in writing. When they have finished their work, call on students from each group to summarize their responses. Discuss the responses, especially the responses to questions 4 and 5.

1. *If Kirsten and Brad Moore sell their timber and invest the money they earn from the sale, it will help them pay for college expenses and their retirement.*

2. *Friends and neighbors in the area have grown accustomed to seeing the Moores' wooded land. It is a feature of the local landscape that they find attractive.*

3. *If Kirsten and Brad Moore don't cut their timber, they will give up the money they could earn by investing the proceeds of the timber sale. This might amount to $12,000 to $20,000 per year.*

4. *This case is similar to the case of Luke Seedy and Friendly Jack Salvage in that each case involves a property owner who is called upon to consider a proposal somebody else makes about how to use the property.*

5. *This case differs from the other case in that the friends and neighbors of Kirsten and Brad Moore do not propose to pay anything for the use they want to make of the Moores' property. They want to have that use, but they don't want to buy it.*

I. Summarize the lesson to this point. In deciding how to use their property, property owners weigh the costs and benefits of the alternatives available to them. If somebody proposes a use of the property that would impose a cost on the owners, the owners might well resist — as Kirsten and Brad Moore did. But the property owner might take a different view if the person making the proposal also offers to pay — as Friendly Jack Salvage did — for the property use he or she wants to obtain. The incentives would be different then. The property owner might agree to give something up, but she or he also would get something in return. The deal might seem to amount to a fair exchange, beneficial to both parties, rather than something to be resisted.

J. How might these ideas apply to other cases involving environmental goals and contested uses of privately owned land? Tell the students that one such case, involving wolves and ranchers, arose late in the 1980s in some Western states including Idaho and Montana. **Distribute a copy of Activity 15.2** to each student. Divide the class into groups of two or three. Assign the groups to read the activity, discuss the questions it poses, and respond in writing to those questions. When the groups have finished their work, call on students from each group to summarize their responses. Discuss the responses, emphasizing the crucial role played by costs, benefits and incentives in the dispute over the wolves.

1. *Ranchers sometimes shot and trapped wolves because wolves sometimes ate their livestock. The losses were costly.*

2. *If the livestock killers had been dogs owned by neighbors, the ranchers could have sued for damages. But wolves are wild animals. Nobody really owns them, and the ranchers therefore had nobody to sue.*

3. *Many outdoor enthusiasts — hikers, campers, photographers and others — wanted ranchers to tolerate wolves as wolf packs began to return to northern Montana, Idaho and other states.*

4. *Initially, the ranchers had no incentive to hold back. If they agreed to allow the wolves to use their land (and perhaps their livestock), they would suffer losses for which nobody would pay compensation.*

5. *Hank Fischer's project created a new incentive, encouraging ranchers to tolerate the wolves. It said, in effect, "Let's make a deal. You hold back on killing wolves. In exchange for that, the Defenders of Wildlife will pay you for any live-*

stock of yours that the wolves kill."

6. *Hank Fischer would agree with Kirsten Moore's statement: "If you want it, buy it." His project enabled defenders of wolves to do just what Kirsten Moore recommended. The Defenders of Wildlife wanted to create a safe habitat for wolves, and they bought the safety the wolves needed by paying ranchers to provide it. It was, for parties on each side, a voluntary exchange.*

K. As a point of transition, explain that the transaction referred to in Activity 15.2 — wolf safety in exchange for compensation for losses — did not involve any search for profits. The Defenders of Wildlife is a non-profit organization; it was not seeking to make money by helping the wolves. And the payments to ranchers were intended to compensate them for losses, not to provide them with extra money over and above their costs. But the ideas illustrated in Activity 15.2 also apply in certain cases in which owners of private property do things to help the environment — and make a profit in the bargain. How could that be? How could anybody "sell" environmental quality for a profit? If you did want to sell it, what sort of a shop could you open up?

L. **Distribute a copy of Activity 15.3** to each student. Assign the students to read the Activity and, working again in groups, discuss and respond in writing to the questions it poses.

1. *It's not clear exactly what Tom Milesnick's reasons were. Maybe he just wanted to restore the creeks for his own personal satisfaction. Maybe he was looking ahead to a time when restored creeks might enable him to start up a pay fishery on his land.*

2. *The Milesnicks never had expressed a "Keep Out" attitude toward their property. They did not object to people fishing in their creeks. But by about 1990 the creeks had begun to deteriorate as a result of overgrazing by cattle on nearby ranches. More and more people fishing in the creeks might cause further damage.*

3. *They had checked out other pay fisheries in the area, and they knew from their own experience that fly fishing had become very popular.*

4. *Tom Milesnick's restoration of the creeks was good for business. His work resulted in more fishable water.*

5. *Tom Milesnick's restoration of the creeks was good for the environment. His work resulted in improved water quality, improved vegetation and improved habitat for insects and trout. His plan for controlled access to the creeks helped to protect against over-fishing. And the revenue he earned provided him with money for upkeep and more restoration in the future.*

6. *The anglers who paid to fish in the Milesnicks' creeks would agree with Kristen Moore's remark: "If you want it, buy it." The anglers wanted an environment well suited for trout fishing. The Milesnicks supplied such environment, and the anglers paid to use it.*

CLOSURE

Display Visual 15.2 and state the mystery that has been central to this lesson: How could private property and profits play any positive role in environmental policy or action? Call on students to solve the mystery by reference to what they have learned about private-property ownership, costs, benefits, incentives and voluntary exchanges. Answers should reflect points summarized below.

- *Owners of private property make decisions about how to use their property.*

- *In making decisions, they weigh anticipated costs and benefits.*

- *If they face pressure to use their property in a way that will impose costs on them, they may resist, even when the issue at stake has to do with environmental quality.*

- *Resistance is less likely when environmental quality is approached as something to be produced through voluntary exchanges between the people who demand it and the people who supply it. Then owners of private property receive something in return for whatever they give up in using their property to enhance environmental quality.*

- *Because many people are willing to pay for experiences associated with environmental quality, owners of private property sometimes earn profits by supplying experiences of that sort to anglers, hunters, hikers, bird-watchers and others. The profit motive in these cases encourages property owners to take action that will improve the environment.*

ASSESSMENT

Multiple-Choice Questions

1. Jones lives in a pleasant residential neighborhood. Squirrels in his backyard chew on his telephone lines, shorting out his Internet connection. Jones is angry. He wants to sue somebody. What is his problem?

   a. The Endangered Species Act makes it a crime to sue squirrels.

   b. He can't prove which squirrel is the culprit.

   c. ***Nobody owns the squirrels, so there is nobody Jones can sue.***

   d. Squirrels can only be sued in small claims court, and even if Jones won his case there he would not be awarded much money in damages.

2. If a business owner seeks to increase profits by taking short cuts in disposing of waste, the environment surrounding the business is especially likely to be harmed if

   a. ***nobody owns the affected area.***

   b. the affected area is owned by a local law firm.

   c. the affected area is fragile, with only one-half inch of topsoil.

   d. the waste material is toxic.

Essay Questions

1. In a short essay, tell whether or not you think the following plan would work well to protect songbirds. Explain your conclusion by discussing the costs, benefits and incentives that play a part in the plan:

A wildlife organization raises money from its members for use in protecting songbirds. It spends some of this money to produce special collars for housecats. It also buys supplies of cat food in bulk quantity. The cat collars carry a medallion; each medallion has an inscription that says, "Hi, my name is [cat's name], and I stay indoors all the time." The medallions are given away to cat owners at Audubon Centers, county fairs, shopping malls, PTA meetings, and so on. Each cat owner who accepts a medallion signs his or her name on to a special honor roll of people who declare that they love songbirds and promise to keep their cats indoors, where they can't eat birds. The honor roll is published from time to time in local newspapers. Each cat owner who signs on to the honor roll is also given a 10-pound sack of cat food.

The plan would probably create an incentive for some cat owners to keep their cats indoors. They might see a benefit in being identified with other signers of the honor roll as people who are doing their part to help song birds. And they might be happy to receive the 10-pound sack of cat food. Also, in signing on with this plan, cat owners don't incur any new dollar costs. But some cat owners might be reluctant to deprive their cats of outdoor activity, and this anticipation of a non-monetary cost might serve as a disincentive, discouraging them from cooperating fully in the plan.

2. In your own words, explain the meaning of Kirsten Moore's motto: "If you want it, buy it." In your explanation, be sure to tell how that motto applies in the case of environmental issues that involve disputes over how private property should be used.

Disputes over the use of private property arise when somebody wants a property owner to use his or her property in a certain way, even if that use imposes a cost on the owner. Kirsten Moore's position is that, in these cases, those who want to see the property used in that way should, in effect, "buy" the use of the property by paying the owner for whatever costs he or she may encounter. As applied to the case of wolves that eat livestock in mountain ranges, for example, Kirsten Moore's motto suggests that those who want to obtain safe habitat for wolves should pay ranchers for any livestock losses caused by wolves — thus "buying" the safe habitat needed for wolf restoration.

VISUAL 15.1

USING LAKE SUPERIOR AS A FREE WASTE-DISPOSAL DUMP

- Mining companies extracted large quantities of iron ore from the Mesabi Range in northern Minnesota throughout the first half of the twentieth century.

- When the supply of high-grade iron ore ran low after World War II, some mining companies shifted over to producing taconite, a low-grade version of iron ore.

- Taconite plants located along the north shore of Lake Superior sometimes used the lake as a receptacle for waste materials they generated as they processed ore into taconite. The lake was right there — conveniently located — and it cost little to dump the waste into the water. The waste that got dumped included asbestos, a silicate material that can cause cancer in humans.

VISUAL 15.2

COULD PRIVATE EFFORTS IMPROVE ENVIRONMENTAL QUALITY?

Many examples suggest that people seeking profits or their own private advantage have harmed the environment. Since this is so, why shouldn't environmental protection be set aside as a special goal to be sought through government regulation? How could private property and profits play any positive role in environmental protection?

LESSON 15

ACTIVITY 15.1

CASE STUDY 1: IF YOU WANT IT, BUY IT

Name_____

Sarah Birkstad is a pediatrician. Kirsten Moore is a real-estate agent. They have been neighbors in the Piedmont Hills of North Carolina for more than 20 years. Their children played together as youngsters; their husbands are friends and hunting partners. Today Sarah and Kirsten share many interests including gardening and hiking.

Recently Sarah learned that Kirsten and her husband, Brad, have decided to cut and sell the timber on their property. Sarah is surprised and deeply disappointed. She invites Kirsten to join her for lunch so that she can learn more about what she has heard. We look in on them at Sarah's kitchen table, where Sarah and Kirsten are enjoying some home-made turkey-vegetable soup and biscuits. After catching up on family news, they have begun to discuss the timber cut.

Sarah: I didn't know whether I should believe it or not when Diane told me that you planned to cut your trees. I wanted to find out from you what the real story is.

Kirsten: The real story is that we have decided to cut the trees, Sarah. Diane had it right.

Sarah: I didn't want to believe it, I guess. We've always enjoyed walking together in your woods and ours. Many of our friends have, too. Our children camped and built treehouses in those woods. Erik and Brad hunted in them only last month. I hate to think that your portion of the woods will be reduced to stumps and scrap now.

Kirsten: I admit it, Sarah. It's going to look bad for a while. We've both seen clear-cuts in other areas, and the sight is always jarring until new growth begins.

Sarah: You're not going to do a clear-cut, are you?

Kirsten: Not quite. We'll leave some seed trees to the north and west of our house, and among the hardwoods we'll leave some trees to provide nuts and seeds for deer and turkey. But even so, it's going to be a big harvest. It's not going to look the same.

Sarah: I'm not the only one who's going to be unhappy about this.

Kirsten: You're telling me? Brad and I have had phone calls and e-mail messages from people all over the county. Most of them tried to be polite about it, but all of them got around to voicing some pretty strong objections.

Sarah: What did you tell them? Why have you decided to cut your trees?

Kirsten: The explanation isn't very complicated. Our timber is worth about $300,000 right now. If we sell the timber and invest the money, we'll probably earn somewhere between $12,000 and $20,000 a year on the investment. Kiera starts college next fall, and Max isn't far behind. With an extra $15,000 or so coming in every year, we may not have to borrow much money to get those kids through school. And then there's the matter of our retirement. I won't have any pension when I retire, and Brad's pension will be small. We'll need that $300,000 and more when we both quit working.

Sarah: The benefits to you are very clear, but the downside is clear too. No more woods on your side for Brad to hunt in. No views of wooded hillsides, looking south from your deck — or north from ours. No big trees for grandchildren to climb in.

Kirsten: Yes, we really will miss those amenities. It wasn't an easy decision for us. But we had to decide whether we wanted to give up $15,000 a year just now in exchange for some hunting acreage and scenic views. We decided that we didn't. The cost is just too high.

ACTIVITY 15.1, CONTINUED

Sarah: Could anything persuade you to change your minds?

Kirsten: I doubt it — not as a practical matter.

Sarah: What do you mean, "Not as a practical matter"?

Kirsten: Our woods are worth about $15,000 a year to us if we cut the trees. If other people in the area actually wanted to prevent that from happening, they could call us right now — not to protest and lecture us, but to offer to buy the timber rights for $15,000 per year. Then they could relax and do nothing — cut no trees, or only a few scraggly ones — and the woods would be there for them to look at and hike in. But as a practical matter, I doubt that anybody will propose such a deal.

Sarah: I don't suppose so. It sounds a bit crass, suggesting that people should pay you not to cut your trees.

Kirsten: I suppose it does, if you just react to the idea quickly. But the idea isn't strange at all once you think twice about it. Just consider the flip side of the problem. Isn't it a bit crass for other people to think that Brad and I should pay $15,000 a year so that they can continue to look at our woods and hike there occasionally?

Sarah: You wouldn't actually be paying out $15,000 a year if you let the woods go uncut.

Kirsten: Same difference. We'd be giving up $15,000 a year. If other people want us to pass over an opportunity to earn that kind of money, they should buy the opportunity from us. That's how it works in other cases, after all. If you want something of value, you buy it or you rent it. You don't expect to get it for nothing, at somebody else's expense.

Thanks to W. Kaufman, whose article "A Clear-Cut in the Piedmont" (*PERC Reports,* March 2001) inspired Activity 15.1.

Questions for Discussion

1. Why do Kirsten and Brad Moore want to do a timber cut on their property?

2. Why do their friends and neighbors not want them to do a timber cut?

3. What would it cost Kirsten and Brad Moore if they agreed not to do the timber cut?

4. How is this case similar to the case of Luke Seedy and Friendly Jack Salvage?

5. How does this case differ from the case of Luke Seedy and Friendly Jack Salvage?

Lesson 15

Activity 15.2

Case Study 2: But How Could You Buy Protection for Wolves?

Name_____

Throughout North America, wolves were hunted and trapped nearly to extinction by the middle of the twentieth century. Since then, however, wolf populations have begun to recover in Minnesota, Wisconsin and some Western states.

For many outdoor enthusiasts, the wolf is an important symbol of genuine wilderness, and they are thrilled by its recovery. They generally support regulations aimed at protecting wolves. They enjoy visiting special museums and zoos to learn about wolves, and they sometimes purchase goods and services that represent the wolf's mystique. Gift shops in Ely, Minnesota, sell wolf T-shirts, coffee mugs and calendars. Galleries sell oil paintings and photographs of wolves. Resorts offer special outings to give guests a chance to hear wolves howl.

But not everybody loves wolves. Wolves are carnivores. Besides eating deer and moose, they sometimes eat dogs, sheep and cattle. Until recently, livestock owners had no way to recover their losses when wolves killed their livestock. As a result, many farmers and ranchers shot or trapped wolves in the past, and many have resisted efforts to reintroduce wolves to regions near their ranges. At a meeting in Idaho in 1984, one rancher explained his objection bluntly: "It's easy to be a wolf lover," he said. "It doesn't cost anything. It's the people who own livestock that end up paying for wolves."

The rancher's objection highlights a basic environmental issue. Many Americans want to protect wilderness, along with the plants and animals found in wilderness areas. Sometimes they do this by establishing national or state parks and forests, and then the costs of wilderness protection are paid for with tax dollars. But sometimes wilderness protection involves efforts that impose costs on owners of private property. When this occurs, landowners often object on the grounds that they are required to pay privately for benefits enjoyed — but not paid for — by others.

An issue of this sort arose in 1987 as wolves began to return to northwestern Montana, near Glacier National Park. In the summer of 1987, wolves killed livestock in the area; ranchers suffered several thousands of dollars in losses, and they were angry. They wanted to kill wolves. Their anger alarmed many hikers, campers, photographers and other outdoors enthusiasts who supported wolf reintroduction. These defenders of wolves wanted to restrain the ranchers.

At the time, Hank Fischer was working in the area, representing Defenders of Wildlife, a private, non-profit organization. Fischer decided that the most important action he could take to support wolf restoration would be to figure out a way to compensate ranchers for their losses. He sent out a fund-raising letter to several Defenders of Wildlife members in Montana and raised the money he needed to get started.

To raise more money, he commissioned a Montana artist to create posters showing wolves as they might look if they were restored to Yellowstone Park. Proceeds from sales of the posters also went into the fund for compensating ranchers whose cattle were killed by wolves. Between 1987 and 2001, Defenders of Wildlife paid about $175,000 to ranchers for wolf compensation. During that time, the controversy over wolf reintroduction to the area subsided.

The compensation program Fischer started up illustrates an important idea. "My view," Fischer stated, "is that people who support wolf recovery should help pay the costs." Acting on this idea, Fischer found that people who supported wolf recovery were in fact willing to help pay those costs when they were provided with a way to do so. As a result, ranchers had less incentive to kill wolves, and defenders of the wolves didn't need to battle against ranchers.

Activity 15.2, Continued

To put the outcome in different terms: People who demanded the reintroduction of wolves were able to buy what they wanted through the compensation program. And people who supplied something crucial to the buyers — rangeland for wolves — got paid for what they supplied. A conflict ready to erupt died down instead because parties on each side were able to pursue their interests through a program of voluntary exchange.

Adapted from H. Fischer, "Who Pays for Wolves?" *PERC Reports,* December 2001.

Questions for Discussion

1. Why did ranchers sometimes shoot or trap wolves?

2. Instead of shooting or trapping wolves, why didn't the ranchers sue somebody to recover damages for the livestock they lost to the wolves?

3. Who wanted the ranchers to hold back and tolerate the wolves that sometimes hunted on their ranges?

4. Did the ranchers have any strong incentive to hold back?

5. How did Hank Fischer's project change the incentives for ranchers?

6. How would Hank Fischer feel about Kirsten Moore's closing remark to Sarah Birkstad in Activity 15.1: "If you want something of value, you buy it"? Explain your answer.

ACTIVITY 15.3

IF YOU DID WANT TO SELL ENVIRONMENTAL QUALITY, WHAT SORT OF SHOP WOULD YOU OPEN?

Name_____

Just outside Belgrade, Montana, two spring creeks — the Thompson and the Bernhart — flow from an underground source and make their way through the fields of a cattle ranch owned by Tom and Mary Kay Milesnick.

Spring creeks make excellent trout streams. Continually refreshed from underground sources, their water never freezes, and they can nurture large trout. But 20 years ago the Thompson and Bernhart creeks weren't known for spectacular fishing. Few people were aware of the creeks at all. Those who did come to fish were allowed open access to the streams by the Milesnicks. "They had to stop and ask [for permission]," Mary Kay says, "but we let everyone on."

During the 1990s, more anglers discovered the creeks. A Robert Redford movie, "A River Runs through It," had helped to popularize fly fishing, and the Milesnicks recall that more and more people began approaching their land in search of good trout fishing. At about the same time, Tom noticed that the creeks had begun to deteriorate from years during which cattle on nearby ranches had grazed near the streams. The streambeds had become laden with silt. The silt choked off most of the aquatic vegetation — vegetation that fosters a healthy insect population, necessary for a good trout stream. Tom described the situation as bleak.

In 1993, Tom bought a backhoe and began working to restore the creeks to health. He spent six years digging holes, laying rocks, removing sediment, planting streamside and aquatic vegetation and channeling water so fish could spawn. His efforts brought the creeks back to life.

Having worked hard to restore the creeks, at a personal cost of about $70,000, the Milesnicks began to think about how they could limit the public's use of their land. They could cut off public access completely by posting "no trespass" signs, but they did not want to do that. Instead they wanted to allow people in manageable numbers to fish in their streams. They were not sure how to do that.

Then they came upon the idea of pay fisheries. There were pay fisheries at several private creeks in nearby Paradise Valley, and the Milesnicks got advice from a friend and local business owner about how they could establish a pay fishery themselves. Perhaps by doing so they could protect the streams they had worked hard to improve, and perhaps they could earn back the money they had spent on the improvement project.

The Milesnicks opened their pay fishery in 1999, limiting the number of anglers to six per day and charging a fee of $50 per angler (later increased to $75 during peak fishing season). With this system in place, they could be sure that their creeks would not be over-fished and that there would be an inflow of money for use in future restorations and upkeep.

How did it all work out? As of 2002, 500 to 600 anglers per year fished the Milesnicks' creeks, compared to about 1,500 in 1998. What had been a one-mile stretch of fishable water became four to five miles of prime trout habitat. Stream water that had been empty except for silt and rock became a rich environment hosting trout, insects and vegetation. Stream banks that had been barren were lined by cattails, long grass and overhanging bushes. And what once had been a strain on the Milesnicks' time and pocketbook had blossomed into a small business producing revenue of about $30,000 per year—accounting for nearly 40 percent of the Milesnicks' profits for their ranch and fishery operation.

Source: K. Kumlien, "How the Milesnicks Found Markets," PERC Reports, June 2002.

ACTIVITY 15.3, CONTINUED

Questions for Discussion

1. Why did Tom Milesnick spend six years and $70,000 restoring the two creeks on his property?

2. Why did the Milesnicks want to limit but not shut off the public's access to their creeks?

3. What reason could the Milesnicks have had for supposing that people would pay to fish in their creeks?

4. Was Tom Milesnick's restoration of the creeks good for his new pay fishery business?

5. Was Tom Milesnick's restoration of the creeks good for the environment?

6. Somewhere between 500 and 600 people per year fished in the creeks after the Milesnicks opened their fishery. How would these anglers have felt about Kristen Moore's closing remark in Activity 15.1: "If you want something of value, you buy it"?